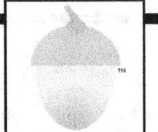

Little Acorn Books

About Early Colors & Shapes

EARLY COLORS & SHAPES SKILLS PRACTICE FUN

by Marilynn G. Barr

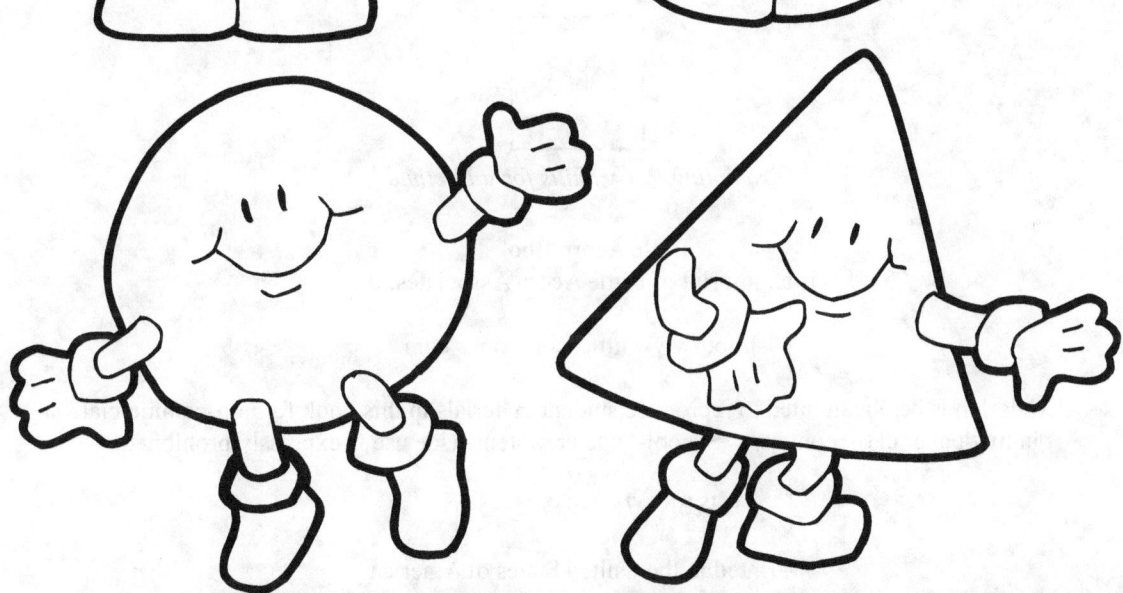

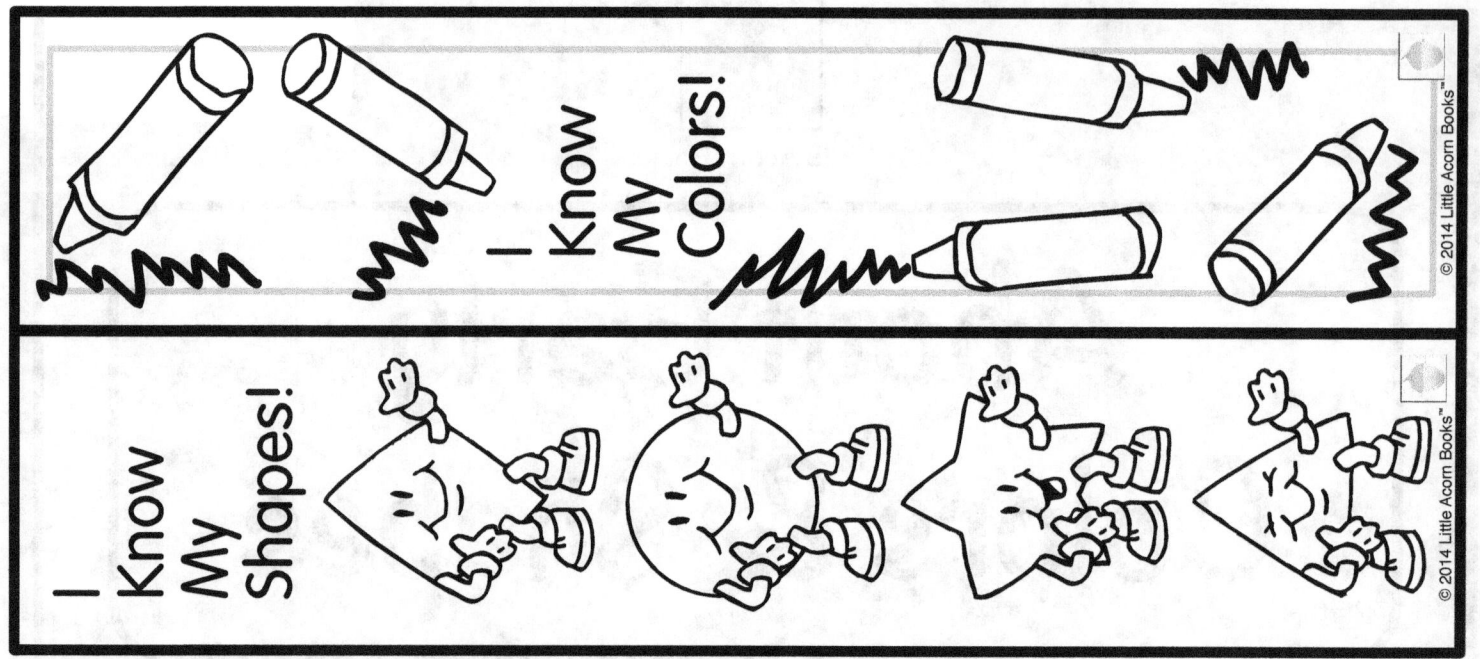

LAB20147P
ABOUT EARLY COLORS & SHAPES
Early Colors & Shapes Skills Practice Fun
Preschool — Grade 1
(*Skills Focus: readiness skills, shape and color recognition, geometric concepts, coloring,
cutting, pasting, matching, lacing, skills achievement awards*)

by Marilynn G. Barr

Published by: Little Acorn Books™

Originally published by: Monday Morning Books, Inc.

Entire contents copyright © 2014 Little Acorn Books™

Little Acorn Books
PO Box 8787
Greensboro, NC 27419-0787

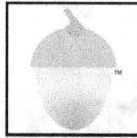

Promoting Early Skills for a Lifetime™

Little Acorn Books™
is an imprint of Little Acorn Associates, Inc.

http://www.littleacornbooks.com

ISBN 978-1-937257-54-5

Printed in the United States of America

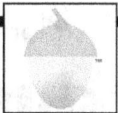

Contents

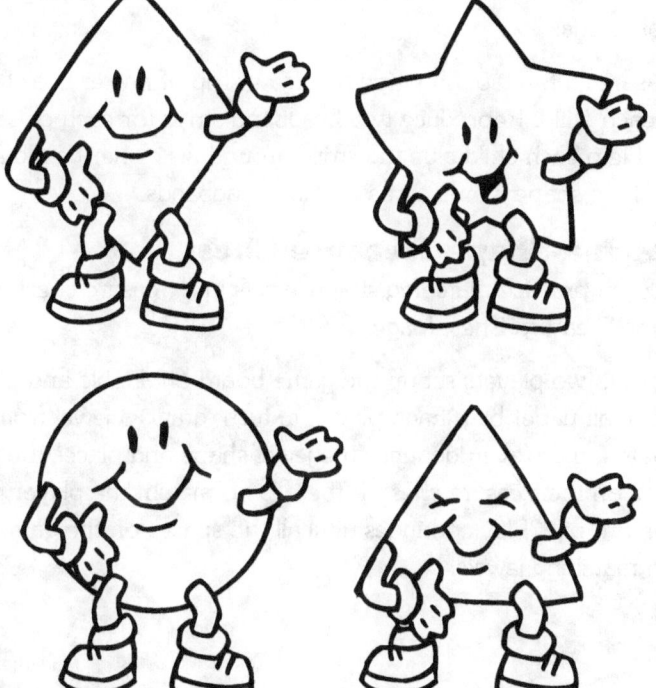

Introduction

About Early Colors & Shapes offers plenty of shape and color recognition, sorting, and matching, as well as fine motor skills practice such as coloring, cutting, pasting, and lacing. The patterns and charts featured include Shape Charts, Shape Tags, Headband Strips, Match-a-Shape Treasure Chest (a match board ga2me), Lacing Cards, Color Boards, Tangrams, Color of the Day Badges, Awards, Take-Home Notes, a More Colors and Shapes chart, and Piglet Paint patterns. *About Early Colors & Shapes* is one of four-book series which includes: *About Early Writing, About Early Math,* and *About Early Reading.*

Shape Charts

Reinforce hands-on shape recognition, cutting, and pasting skills practice with the ten shape charts and matching shape patterns on pages 7-26. Reproduce a shape chart and its matching set of shape patterns for each child to color and cut out. Have children glue shape patterns on shape charts. Mount each child's chart on a sheet of construction paper. Help each child write the shape word along the bottom of his or her picture. Post finished charts on a display board entitled "We Know All About Shapes!"

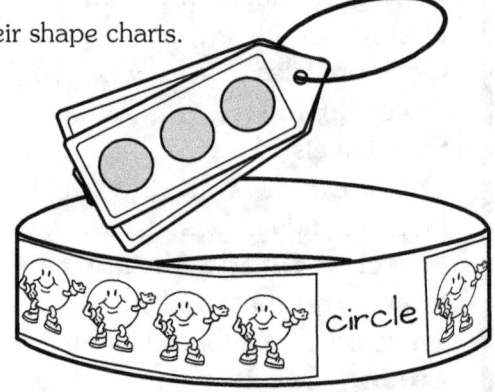

When children finish all ten shape charts, have them decorate construction paper covers. Then help each child staple his or her charts together to form a book.

Set up a work station with containers filled with cotton balls, large buttons, pom poms, glitter, pipe cleaners, craft sticks, and yarn for children to embellish their shape charts.

Shape Tags & Headband Strips

Reproduce oak tag shape tags for children to start a key ring collection. Provide each child with a pipe cleaner to form a key ring. Have children trace the shapes on the shape tags. Then help each child write the matching shape word on the back of the tag. Punch a hole in finished tags for children to thread onto pipe cleaner key rings. Make additional tags for children to program with colors and color words.

Measure, cut, wrap, and tape a narrow strip of poster board to form a headband for each child. Reproduce two headband strips for each child to color and cut out. Help each child glue the strips around his or her headband. Write the matching shape words on assembled headbands.

Match-a-Shape Treasure Chest

Children practice matching shape jewels in a treasure chest as they play Match-a-Shape Treasure Chest (pages 27-29).

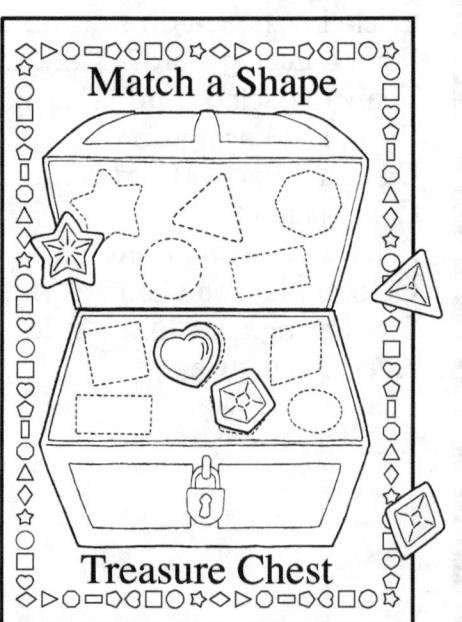

To play, two players set up the game board on a table and place the jewel shapes in a small paper bag. Each player, in turn, draws a jewel from the bag. If there is a match, the player identifies the jewel shape and places the jewel on the correct space on the treasure chest. If there is no match, the player places the jewel in a discard pile. Play continues until all the spaces on the game board are covered with matching jewels.

LAB20147P • About Early Colors & Shapes • 978-1-937257-54-5 • © 2014 Little Acorn Books™

Lacing Cards

Children practice punching holes, lacing yarn, tying bows and knots, and identifying shapes with these full-page, easy-to-cut-out, lacing cards.

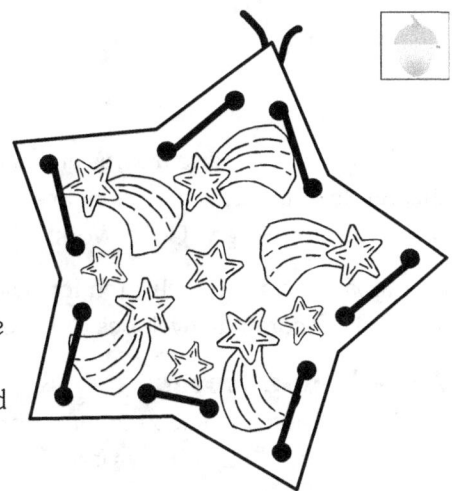

Reproduce lacing cards for each child to color and cut out. Help each child punch a hole at each dot around the perimeter of the lacing card. Measure and cut a length of yarn. Use a twist tie or length of pipe cleaner to form a needle. Thread and secure the yarn in the twist tie or pipe cleaner needle. Show children how to thread yarn in and out of the holes around the lacing cards. Post finished cards on a display board entitled "We Can Cut Out and Lace Shapes!"

Color Boards

Color boards can be used for color recognition practice, to make color journals, or to practice writing with a variety of colored writing instruments (pencils, crayons, markers, glue, and glitter pens). They can also be programmed for use as write-on and wipe-off "horn books." (A horn book is an old-fashioned, hand-held chalk board used by school children for class work.)

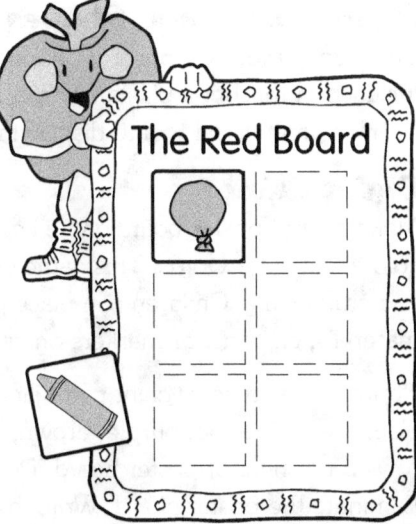

Reproduce, color, cut out, and laminate the color boards (pages 40-46). Reproduce colored construction paper color board cutouts (page 47). Store the color boards and shapes in a decorated gift box. Place the box in a skills practice center. Children can work individually or in pairs to place matching color shapes on each color board.

Reproduce each of the color boards for each child to color, cut out, and glue on a sheet of construction paper. Have children decorate a "My All About Colors Journal" construction paper booklet cover. Help children staple covers and color boards together to form booklets. Instruct children to cut out and glue matching color pictures on each appropriate color board. Place finished color journals on a display table for visitors to see.

Tangrams

Tangram puzzles are great fun for youngsters. Children practice visual discrimination, sorting, and matching skills while assembling tangram puzzles.

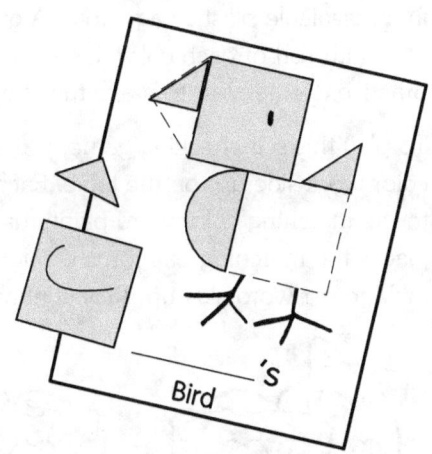

Reproduce a tangram board and puzzle pieces for each child to color and cut out. Have children match and glue puzzle pieces on tangram boards to finish the pictures. Write each child's name on his or her finished board. Mount the finished boards on construction paper for display.

Reproduce and color each tangram board and matching puzzle pieces, then laminate and cut out the boards and pieces. Store each board and matching pieces in a separate manila envelope. Place the tangrams in a skills practice center.

Color of the Day Badges

Reproduce oak tag badges (page 56) with the "Color of the Day" for each child. Have children color and cut out badges. Use cellophane tape to attach safety pins to the backs of badges for children to wear. Option: Provide each child with a folder. Have children glue badges to the fronts of folders. Write each child's name on the front of his or her folder. Children can use these folders to store completed or unfinished work related to the "Color of the Day" on the cover.

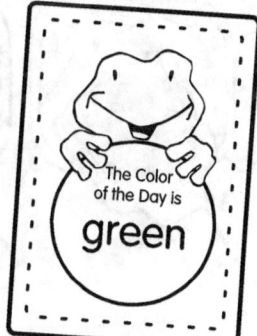

Awards

Children love to receive awards and keep track of their own achievements. Reproduce award booklets (pages 58-59) for children to color and cut out. Help each child assemble and staple his or her booklet. Store all "Good Work!" stickers in a basket. Give children "Good Work!" stickers to glue in booklets as they master each listed skill.

Be prepared to reward children for skills achievement. Reproduce, color, and cut out a supply of awards (page 60). Store awards in decorated envelopes or folders.

Take-Home Notes

Send home notes to keep parents informed about current color and shape skills practice. Reproduce and cut apart a supply of bright-colored paper notes (age 61). Store notes in a decorated manila envelope or folder.

More Colors and Shapes

This handy More Colors and Shapes chart (page 62) displays a few more shapes included in this book plus a few more. Also included on this sheet is a color-in chart, a great visual tool to display in an arts and crafts center.

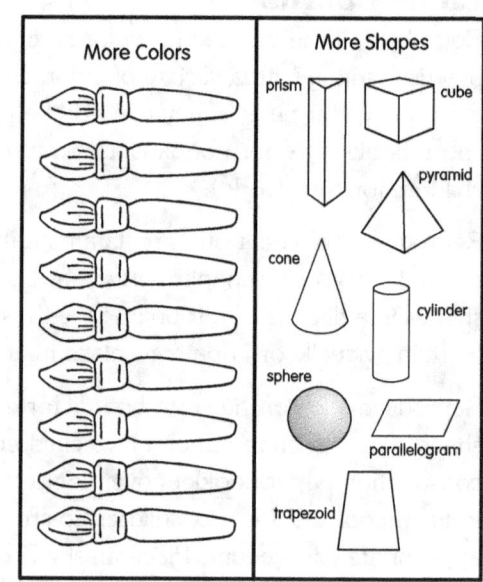

Piglet Paint

Make a large poster board game board for children to practice matching rainbow colors and color words. This game board can also be used to organize an arts and crafts table. Children can place paint jars, containers filled with colored craft materials, crayons, or markers on each matching space on the board.

Reproduce and color eight paint jars and matching paintbrushes (red, yellow, blue, green, orange, purple, brown, and black). Cut out and glue the paint jars in rows on a sheet of poster board. Decorate the border around the poster board. Laminate the poster board. Write the matching color word on the back of each paintbrush. Then laminate and cut out the paintbrushes. Store the paintbrushes in a resealable plastic bag. Note: A game board can include more than one jar or paintbrush of each color. Unusual colors such as turquoise, magenta, etc. can be included for more color recognition practice. Remember to make the matching number of paintbrushes.

To play this self-checking game, players set up the game board on a table. One player shuffles and places the paintbrushes, color word side up, on the table. Each player, in turn, points to and identifies a color on the game board. He or she points to the matching color word paintbrush on the table. Then the player picks up the card and turns it over. If correct, the player places the matching paintbrush, color side up, on the correct paint jar. If incorrect, the player places the paintbrush on the table, color word side up. Play continues until a matching paintbrush is placed on every paint jar.

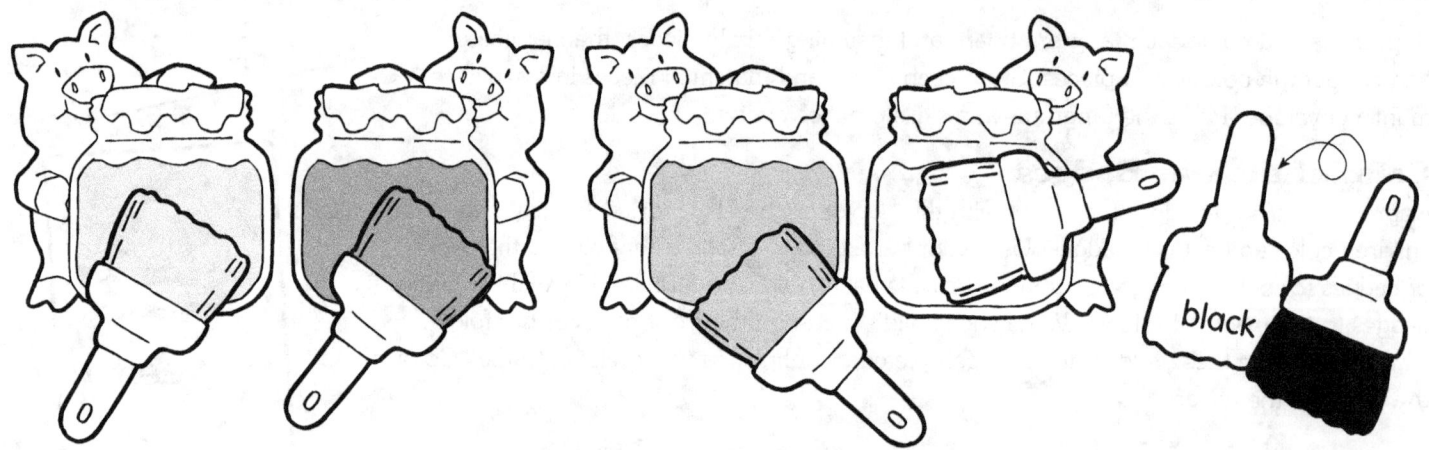

Bubble Pipe

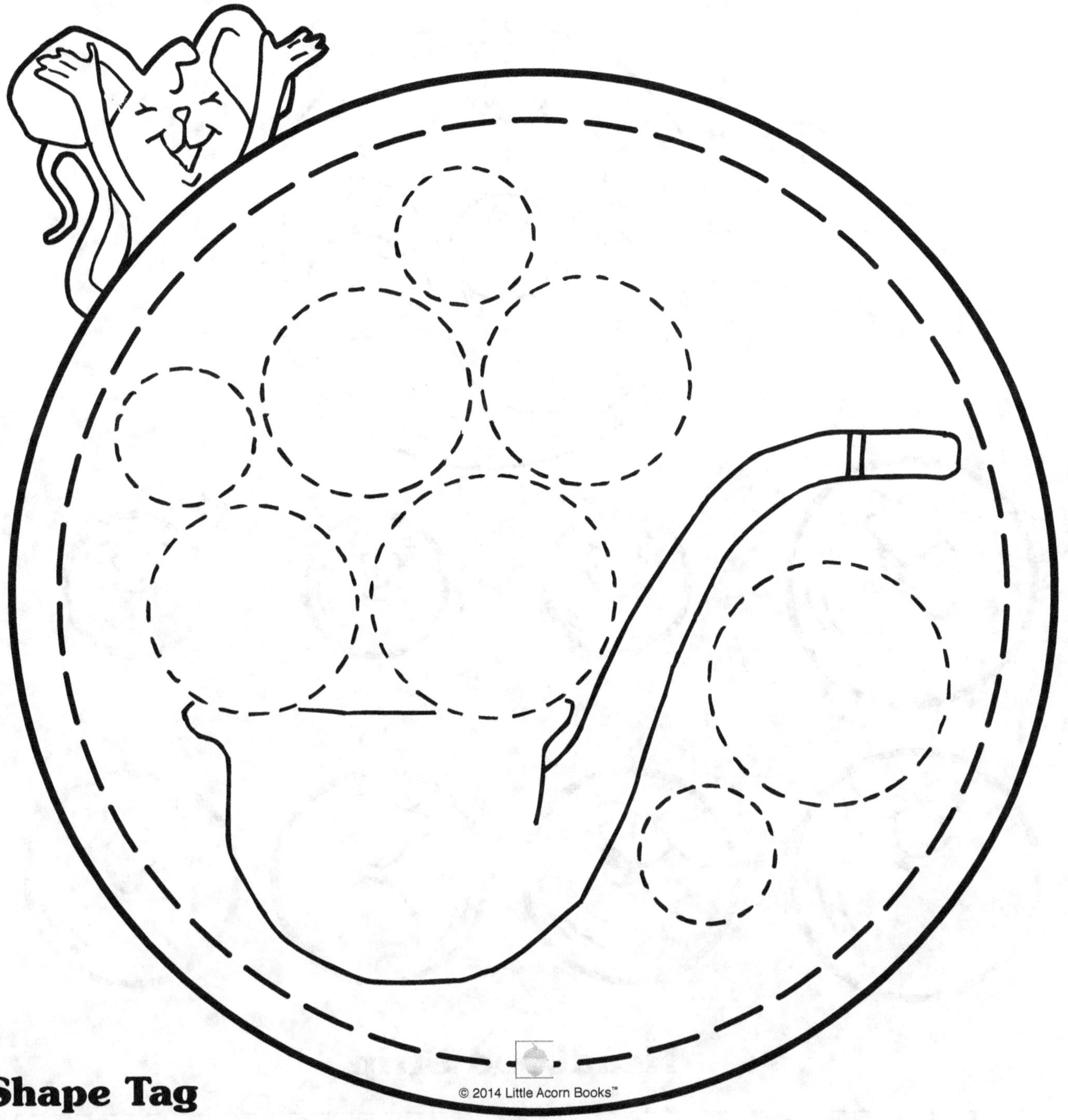

Shape Tag

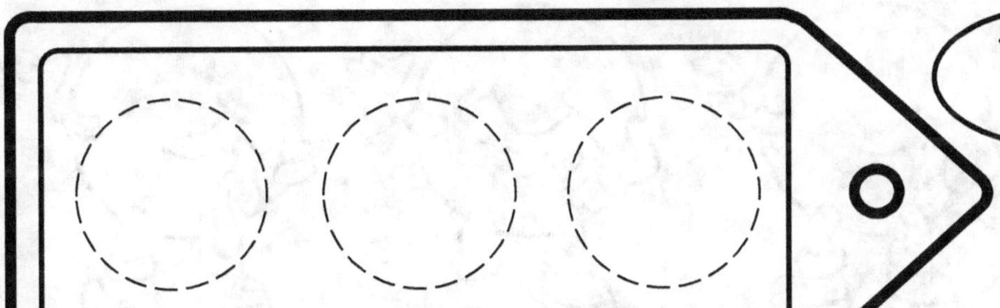

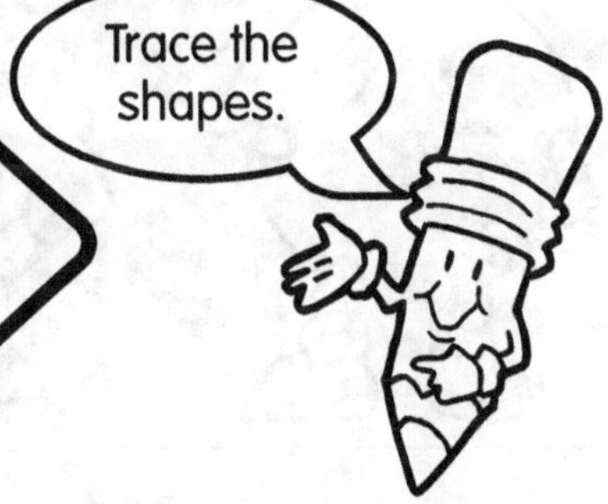

Trace the shapes.

Circle Bubbles

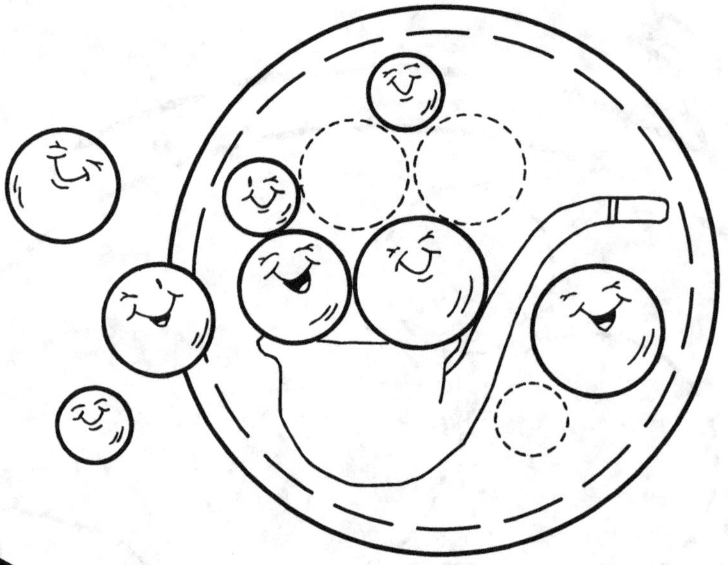

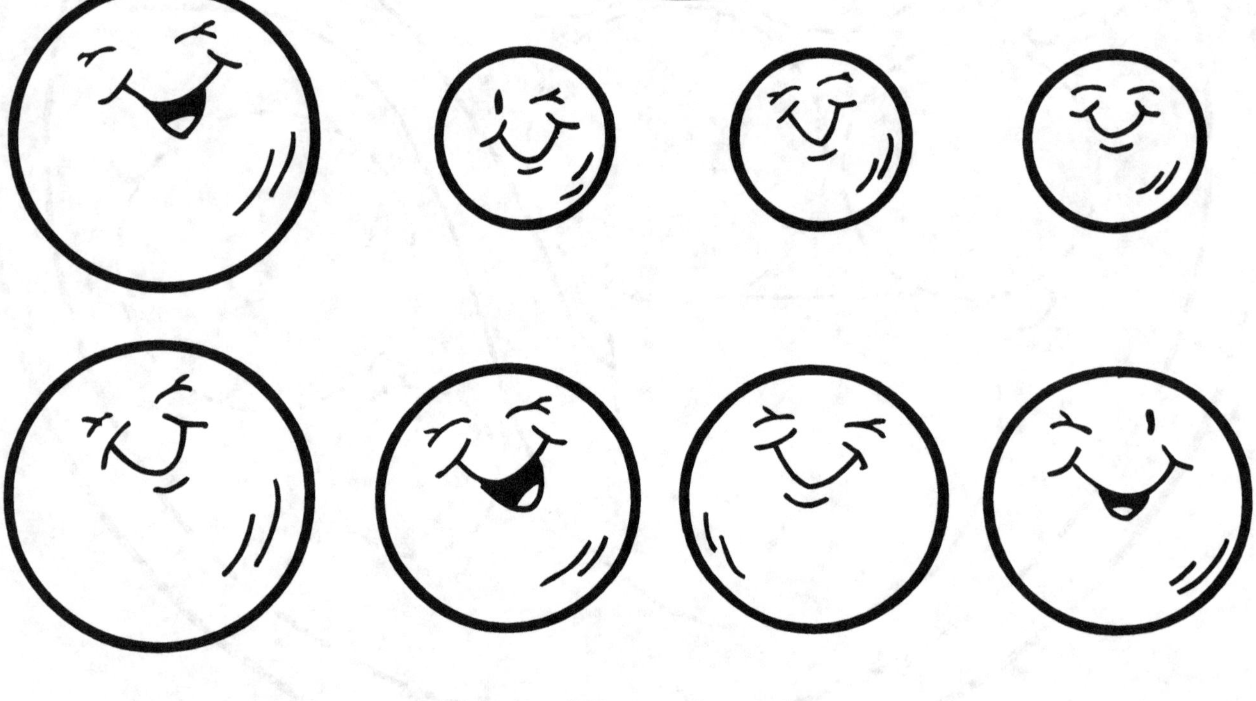

Headband Strip

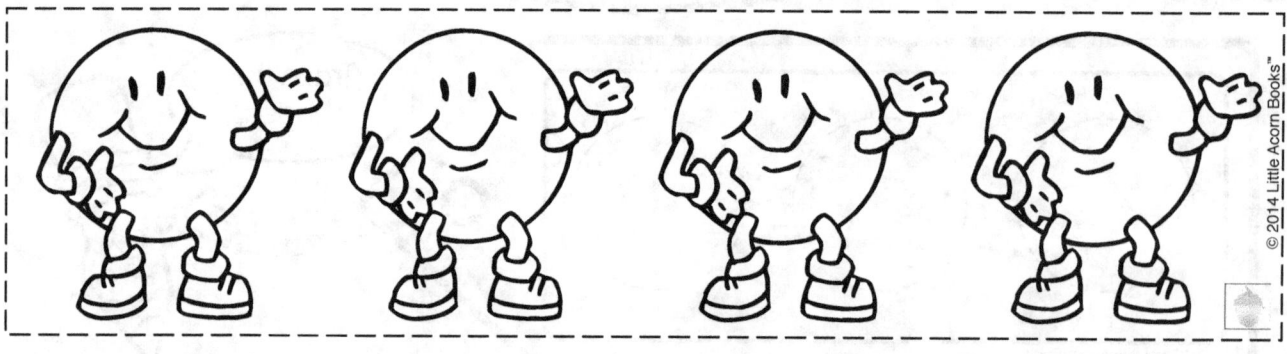

LAB20147P • About Early Colors & Shapes • 978-1-937257-54-5 • © 2014 Little Acorn Books™

Monkey Bars

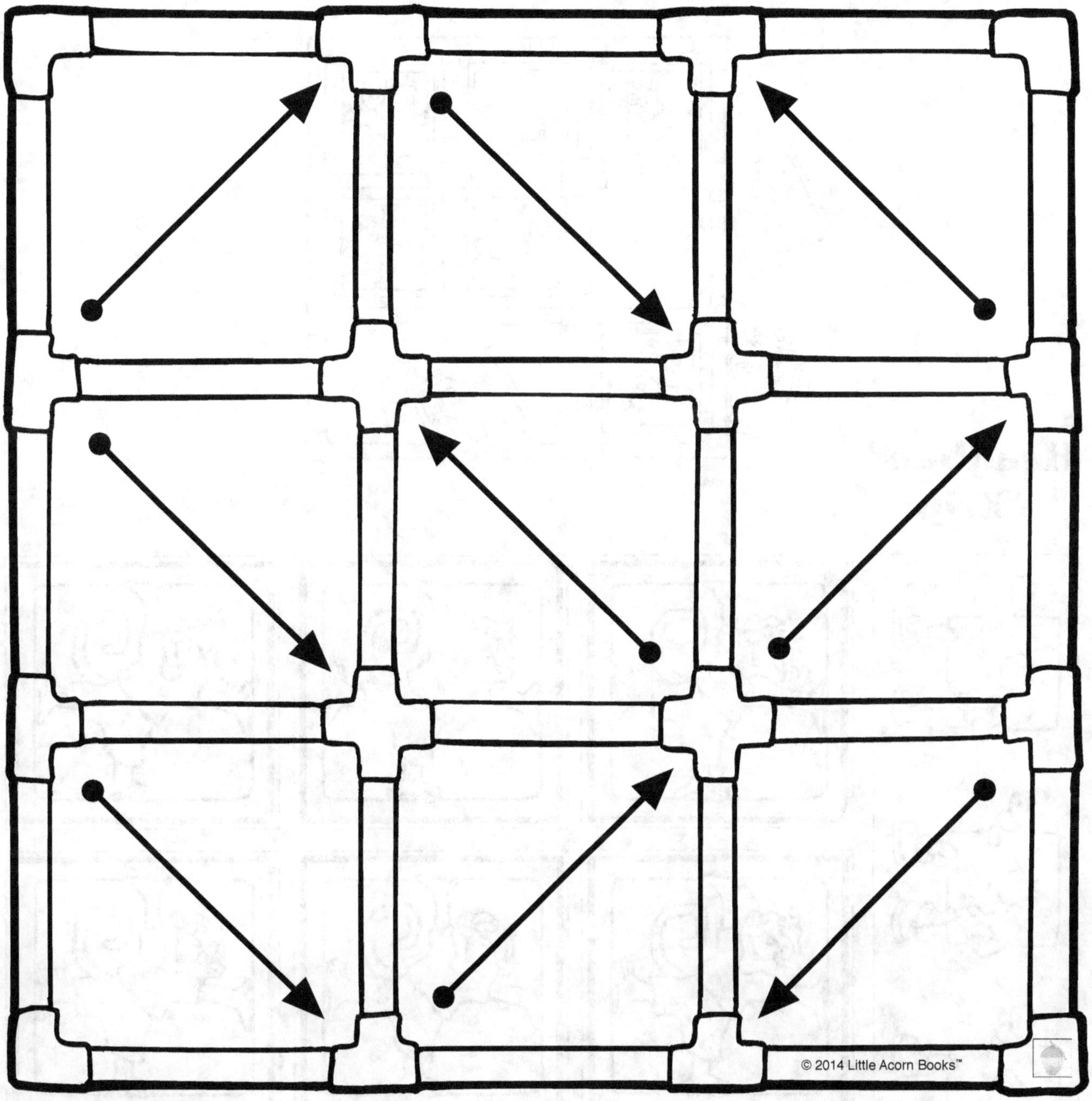

Shape Tag

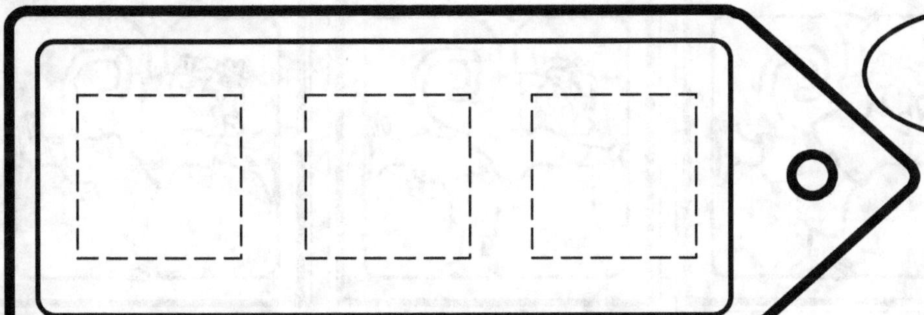

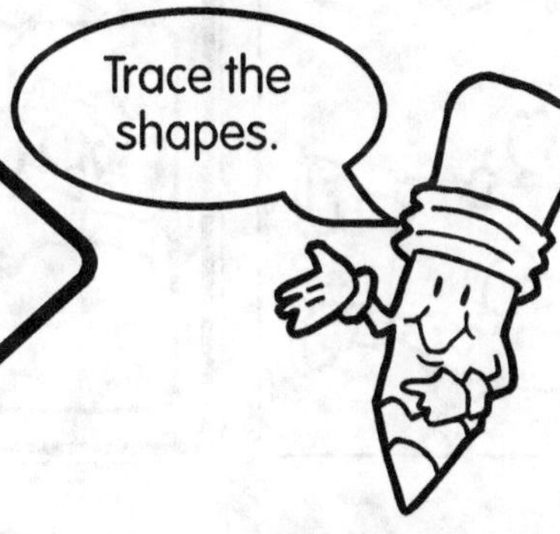

Trace the shapes.

Monkey Squares

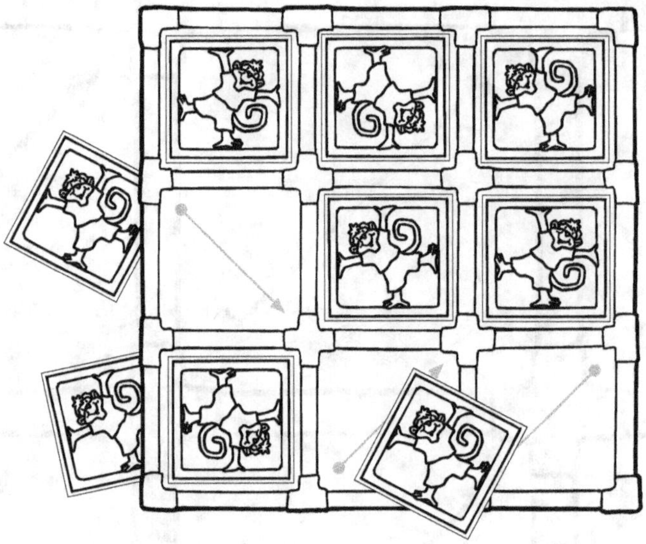

Headband Strip

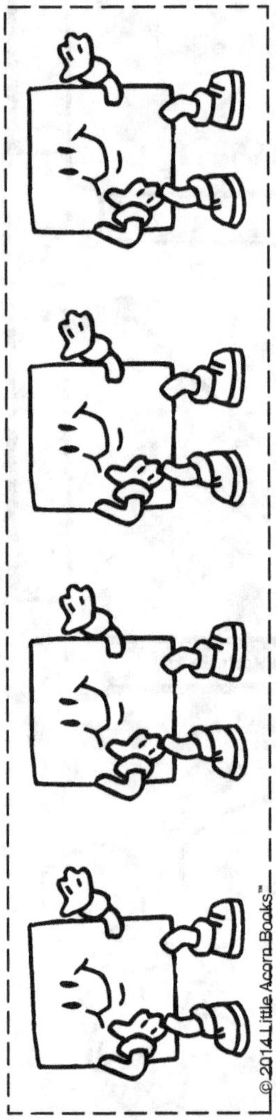

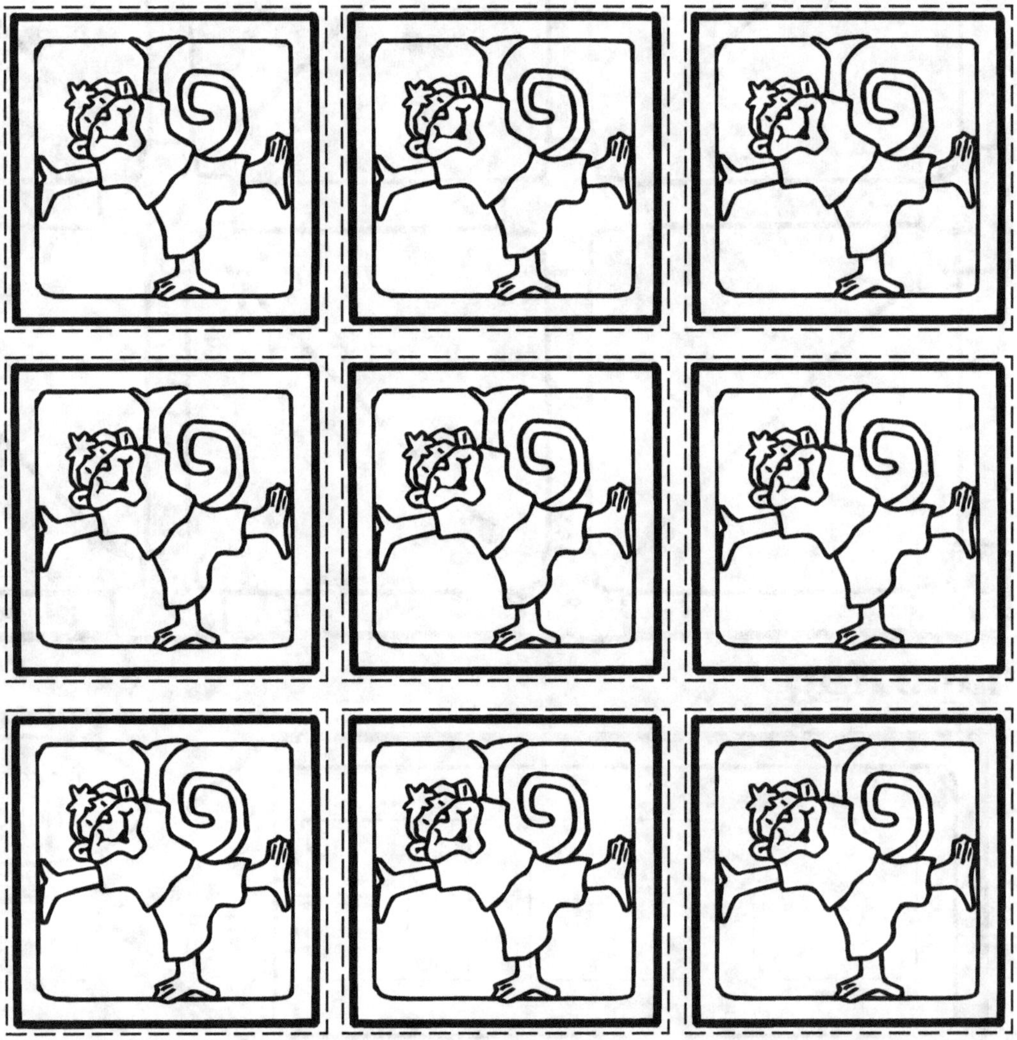

LAB20147P • About Early Colors & Shapes • 978-1-937257-54-5 • © 2014 Little Acorn Books™

Tree Farm

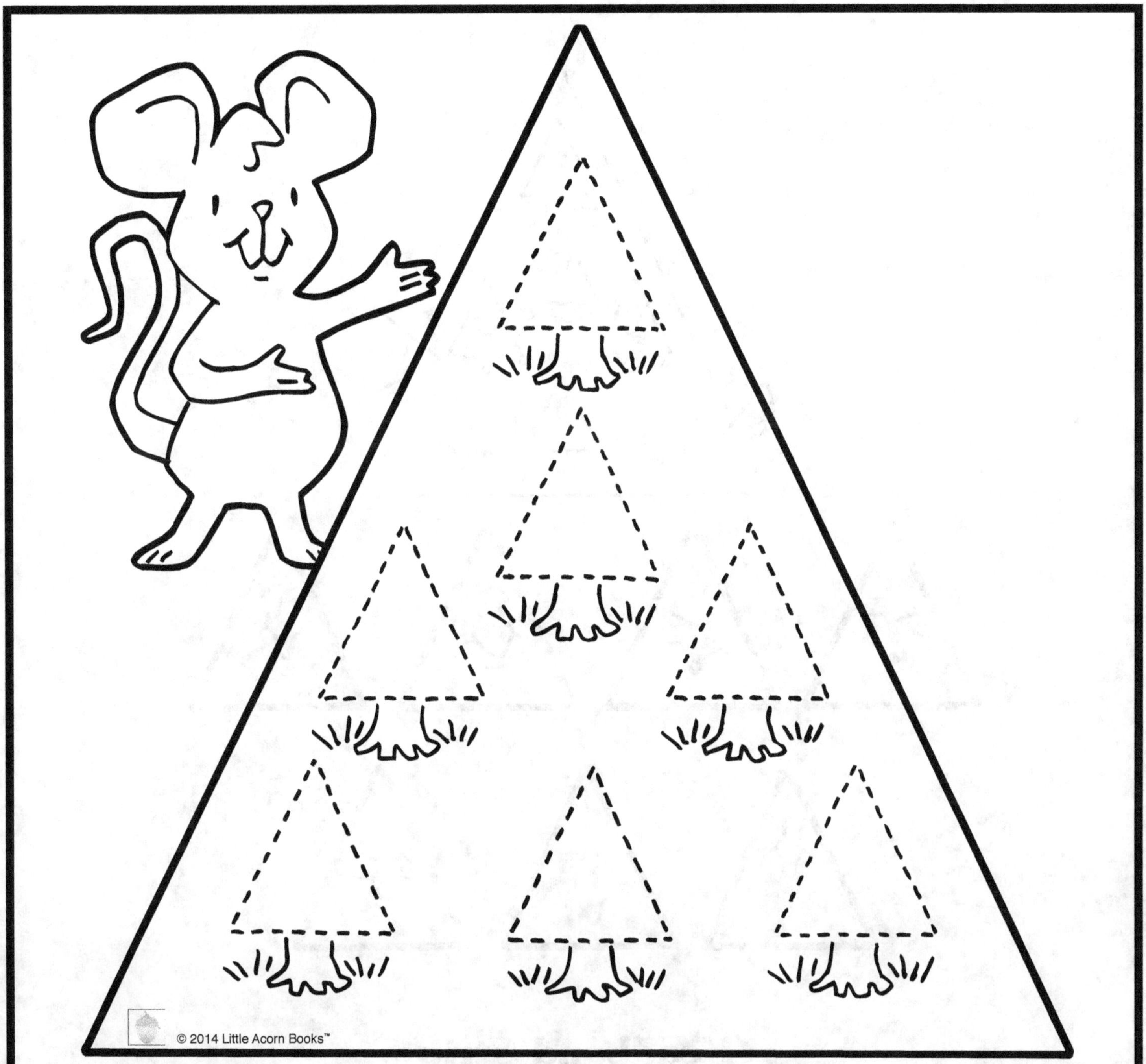

Shape Tag

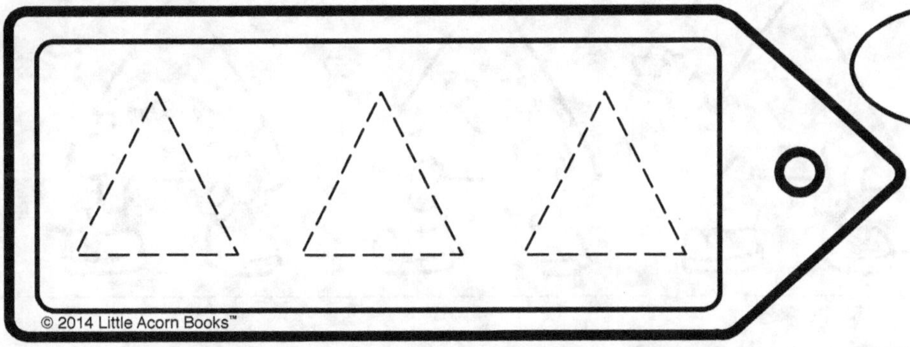

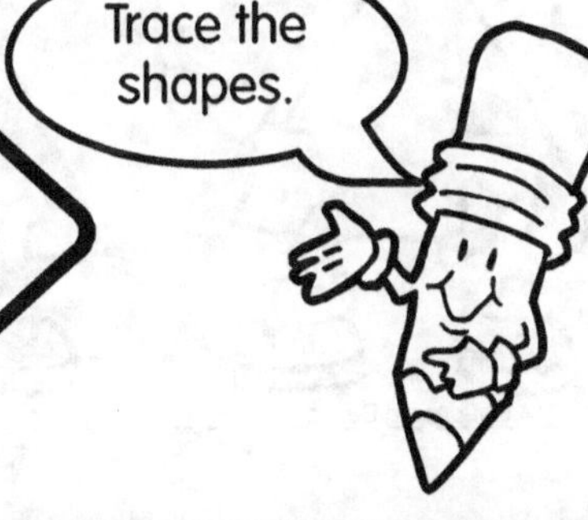

Trace the shapes.

Triangle Trees

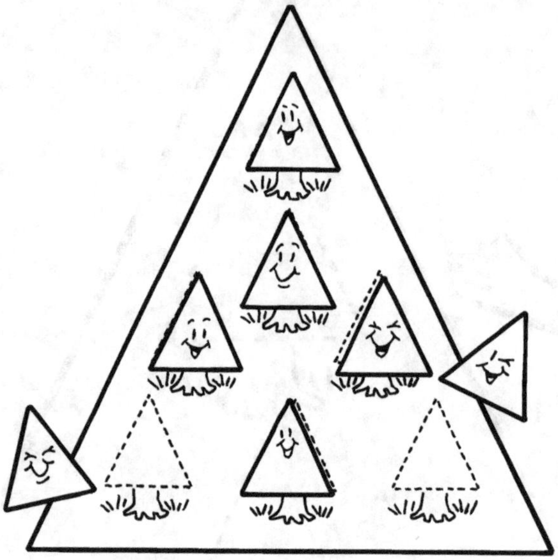

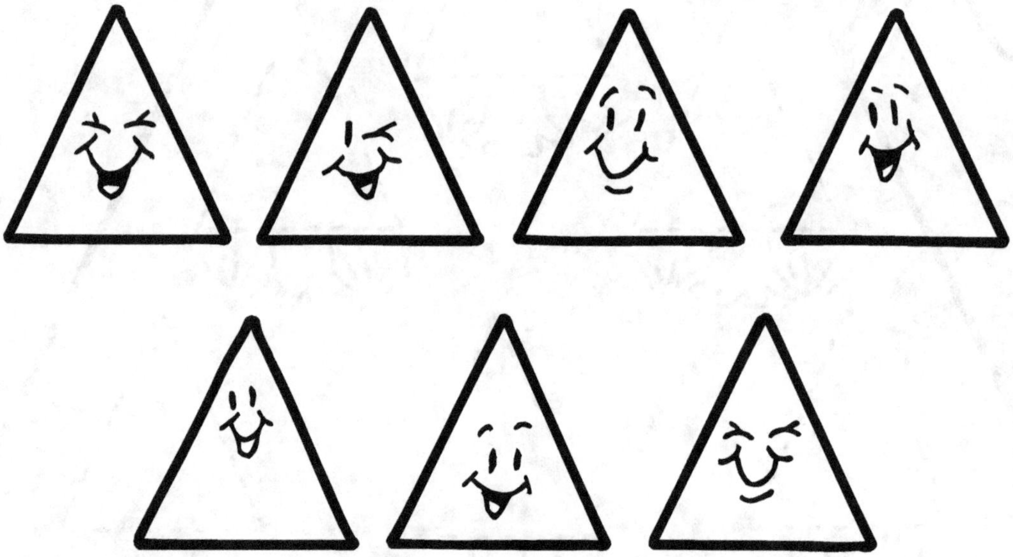

Headband Strip

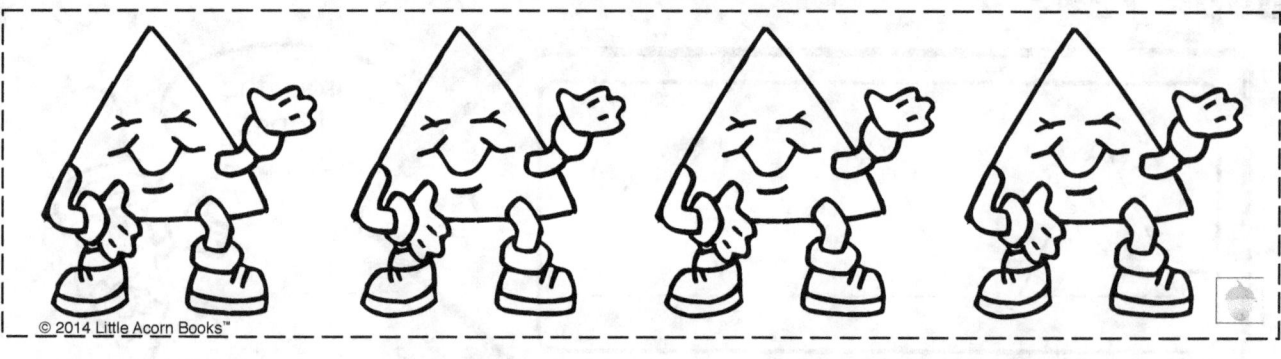

 LAB20147P • About Early Colors & Shapes • 978-1-937257-54-5 • © 2014 Little Acorn Books™

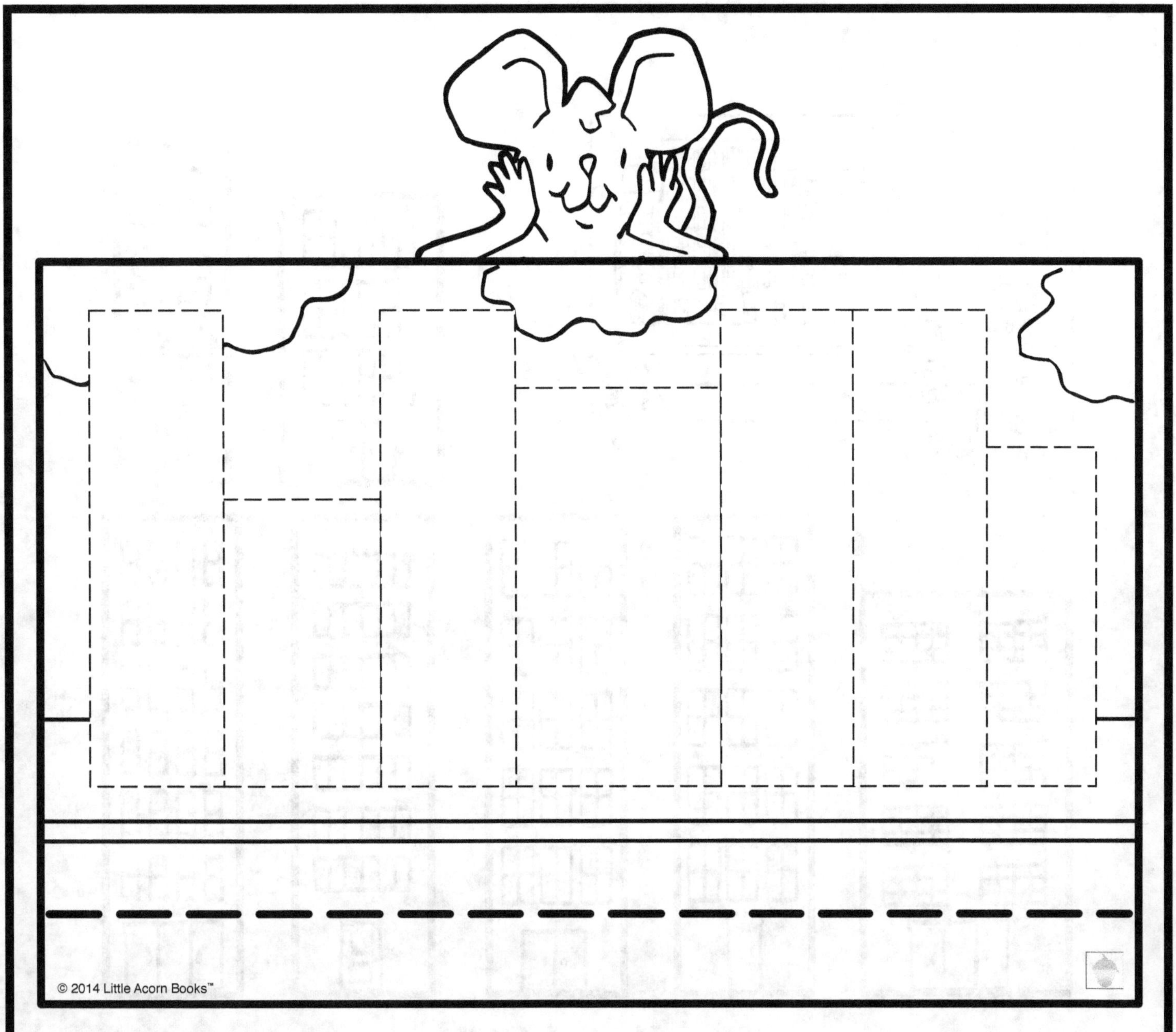

Shape Tag

Trace the shapes.

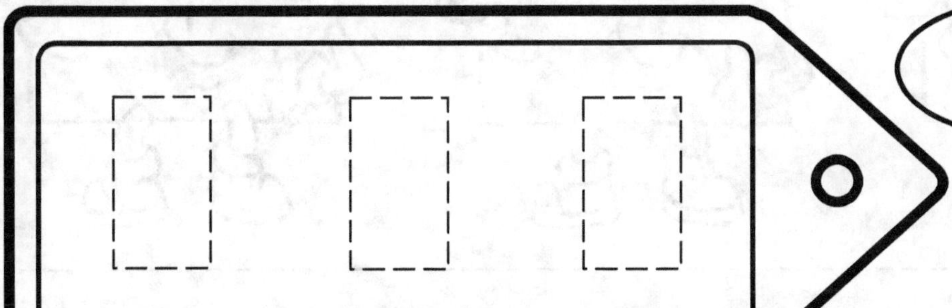

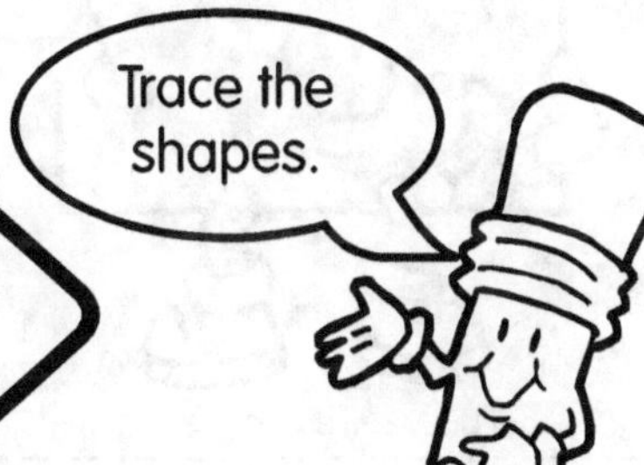

Rectangle Buildings

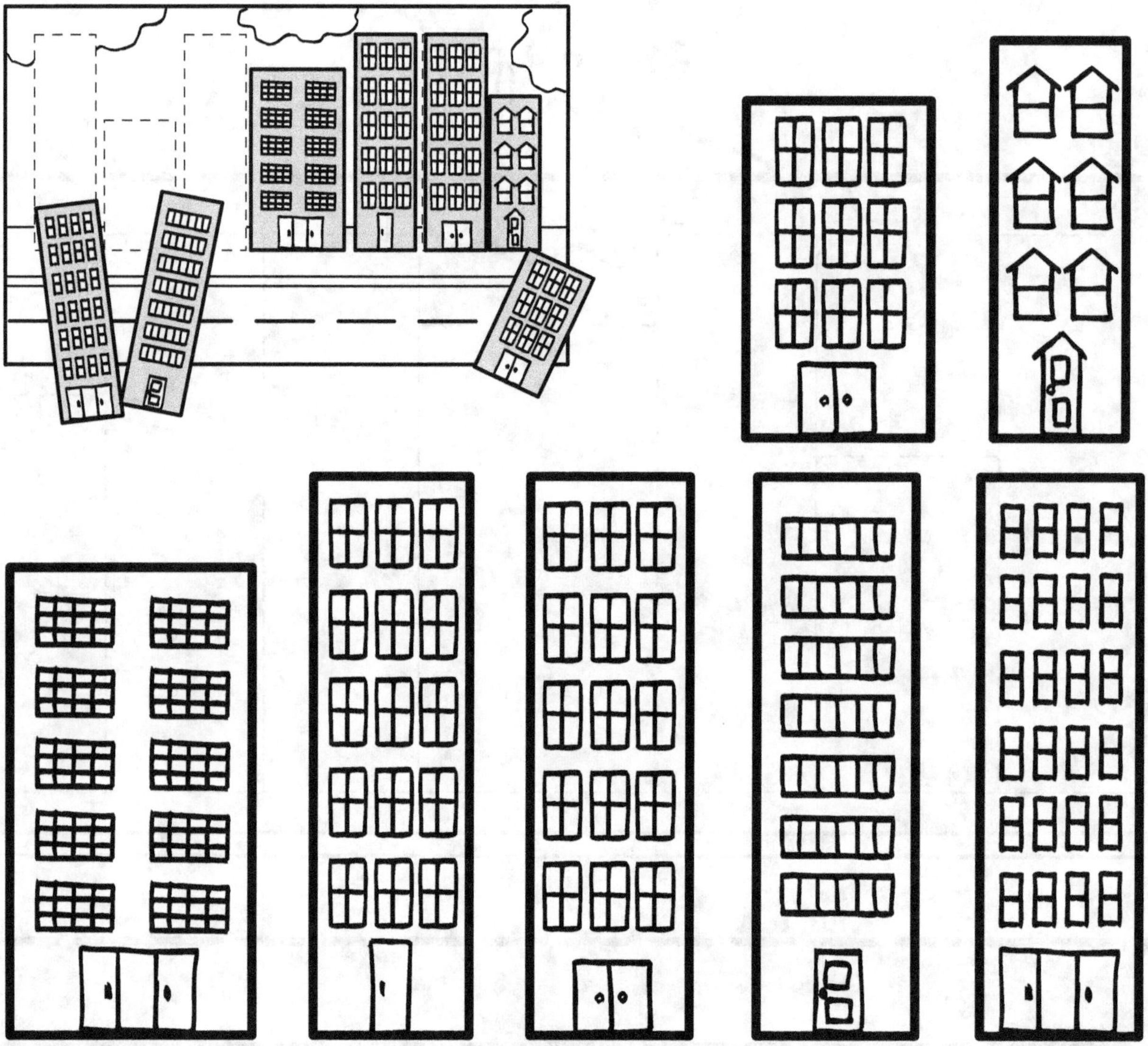

Headband Strip

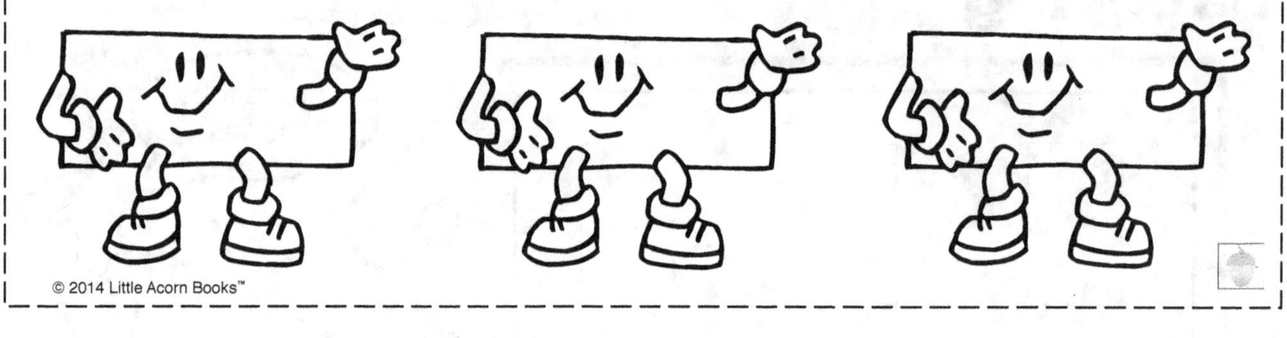

Diamond Quilt

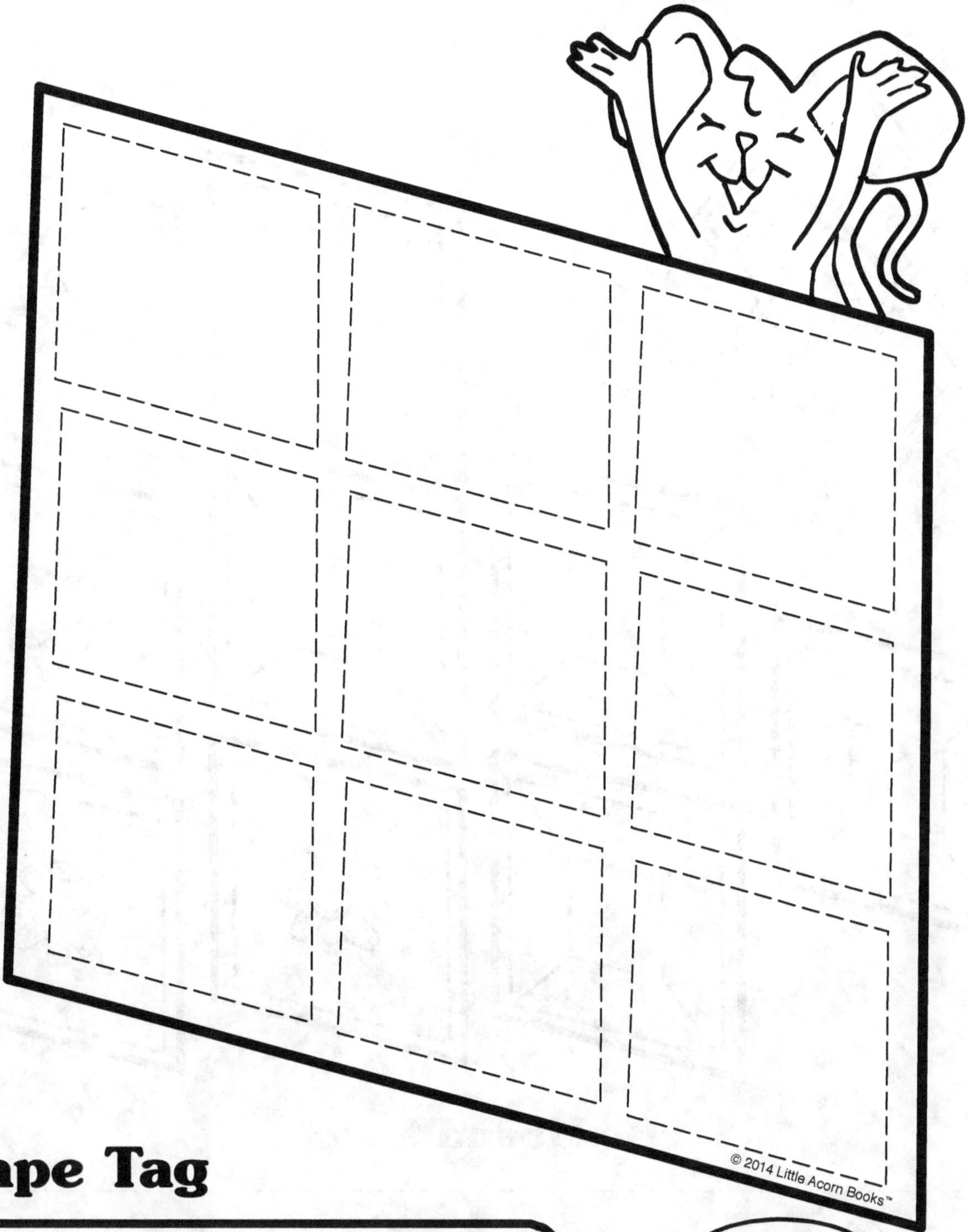

Shape Tag

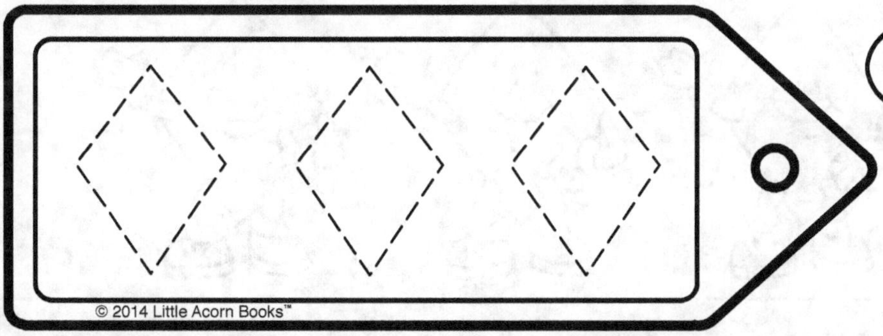

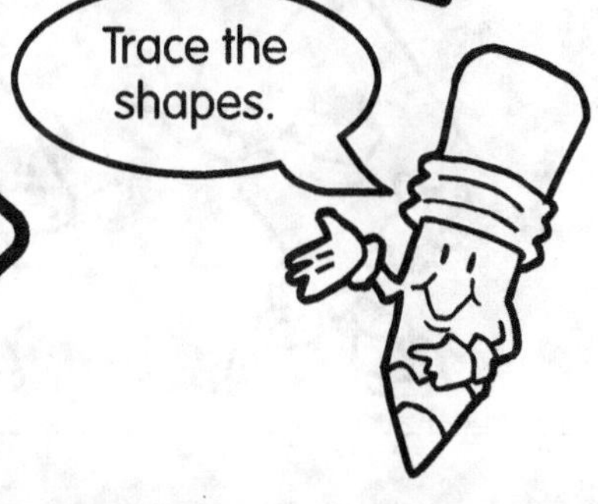

Trace the shapes.

Quilt Diamonds

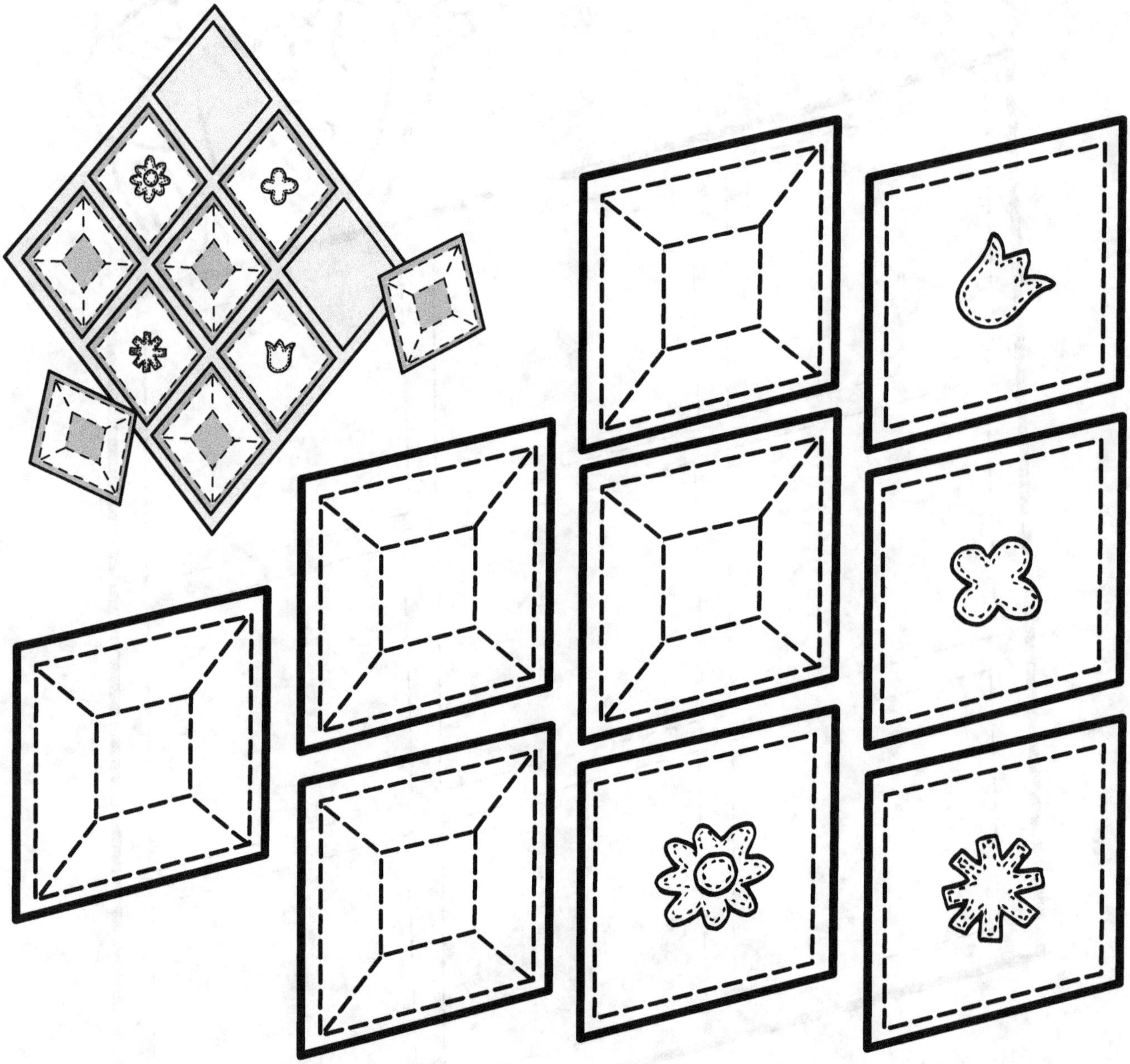

Headband Strip

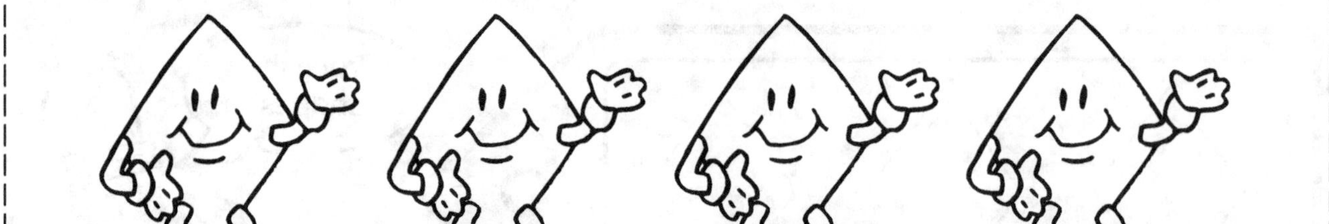

 LAB20147P • About Early Colors & Shapes • 978-1-937257-54-5 • © 2014 Little Acorn Books™

Basket of Eggs

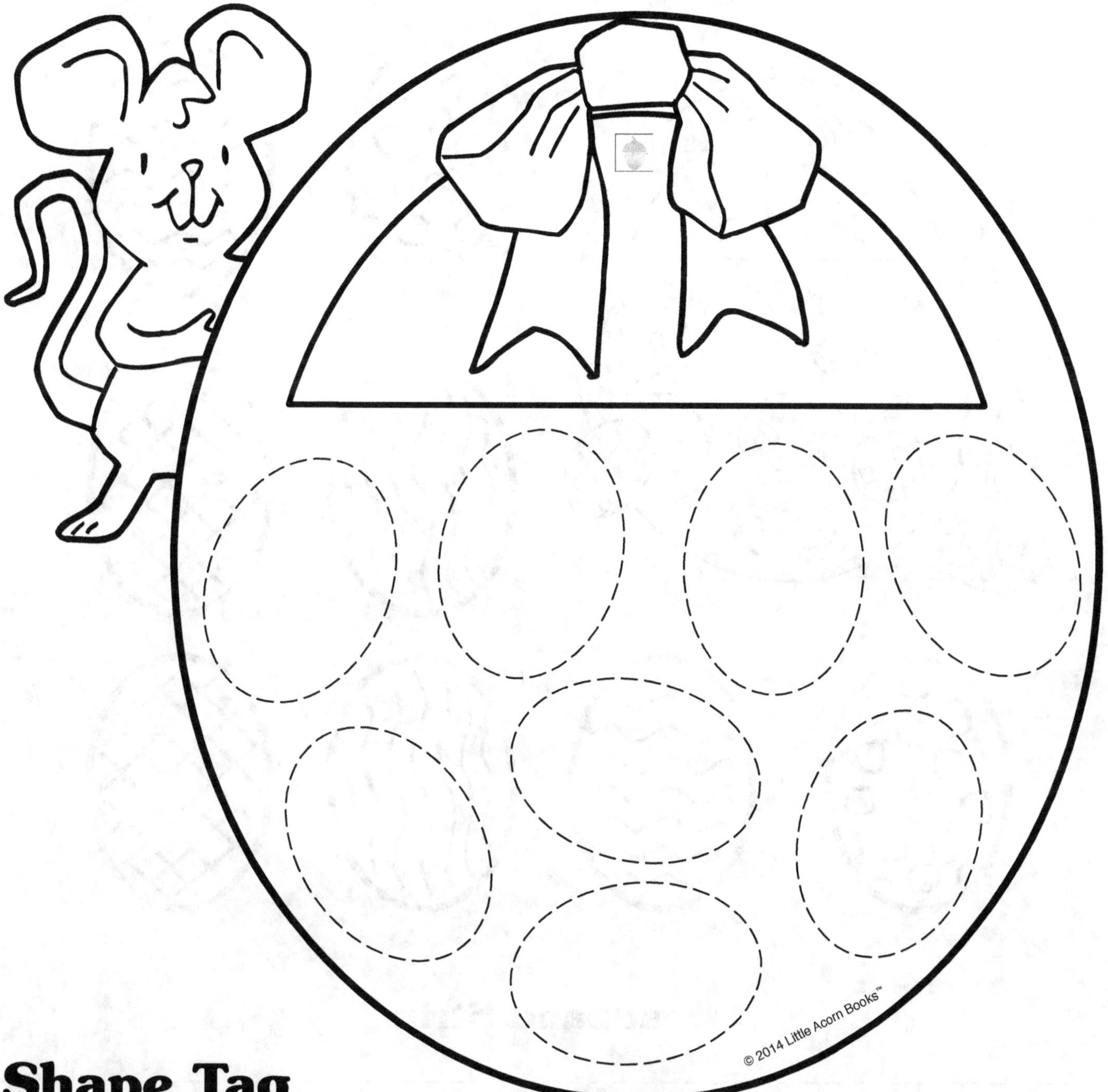

Shape Tag

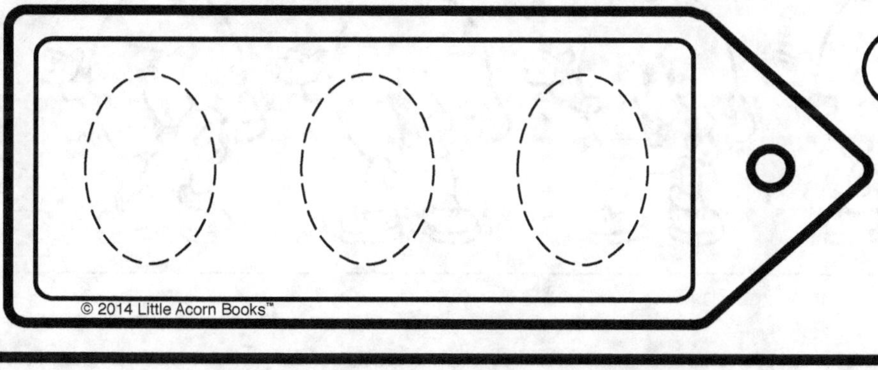

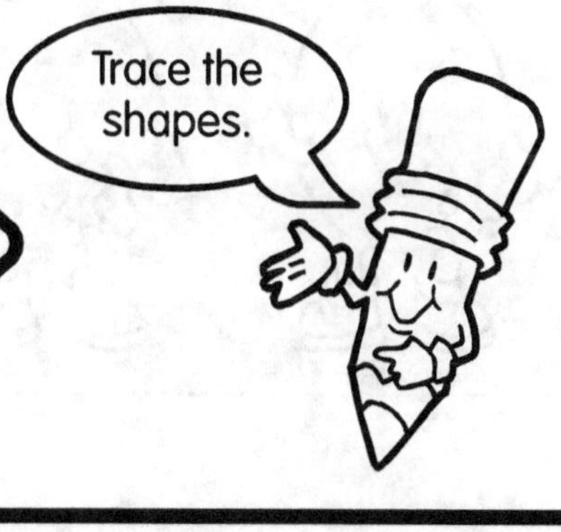

Trace the shapes.

Oval Eggs

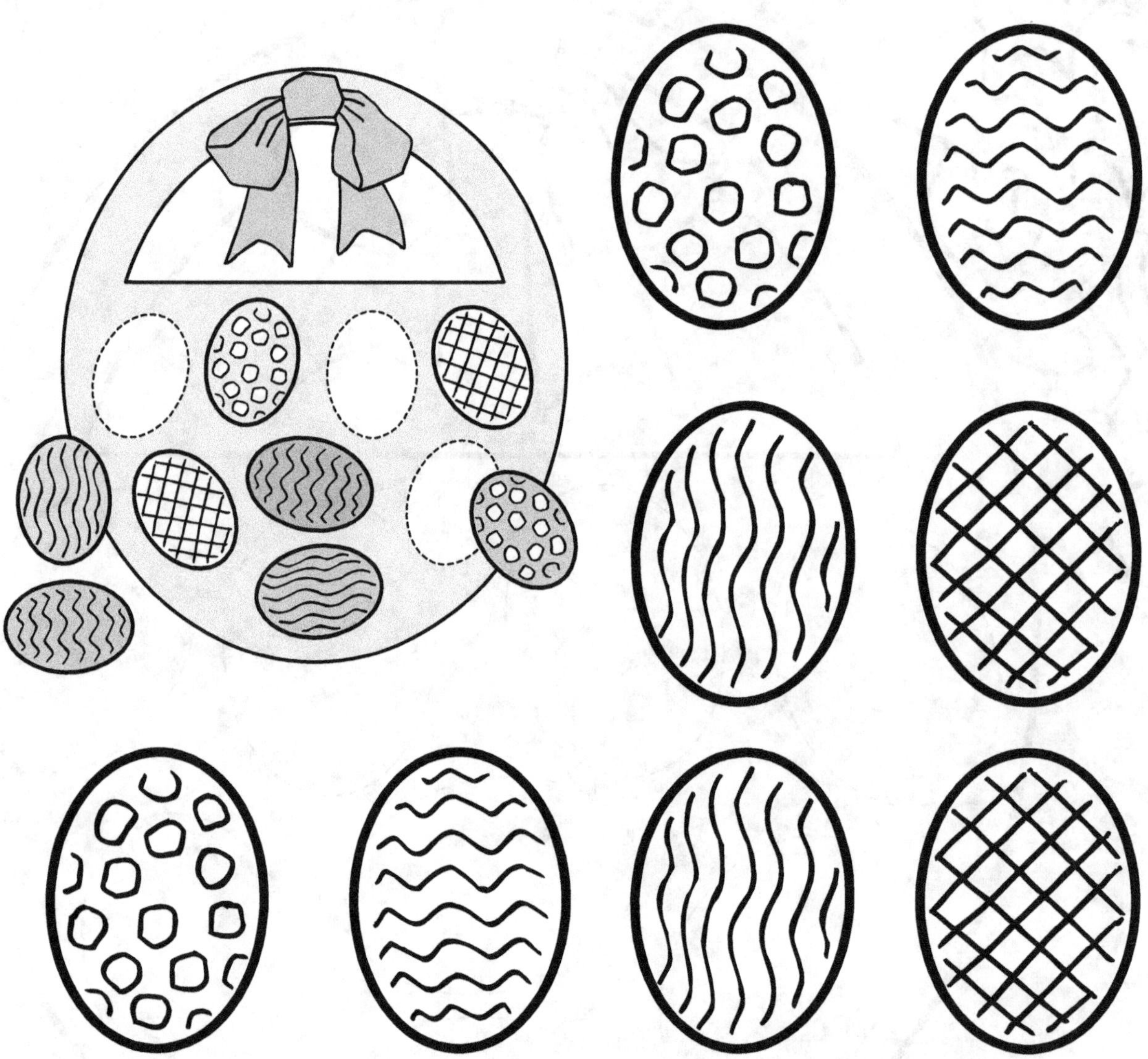

Headband Strip

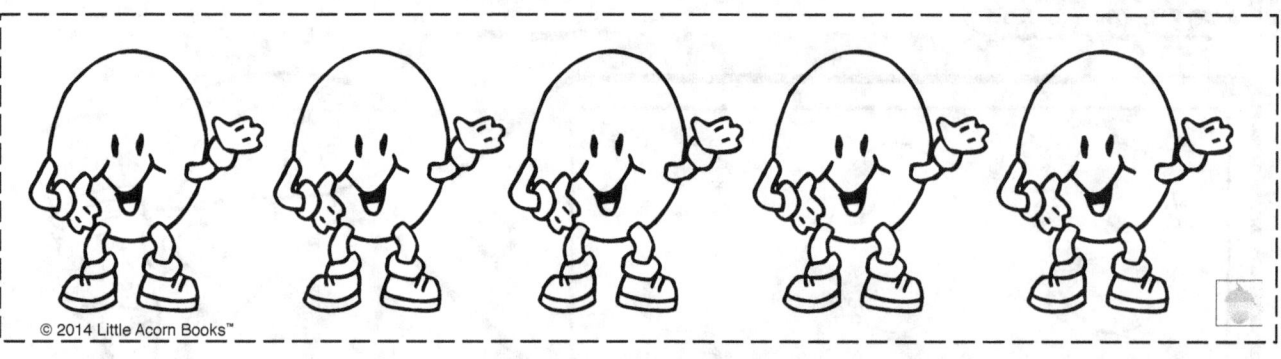

LAB20147P • About Early Colors & Shapes • 978-1-937257-54-5 • © 2014 Little Acorn Books™

Soccer Ball Bag

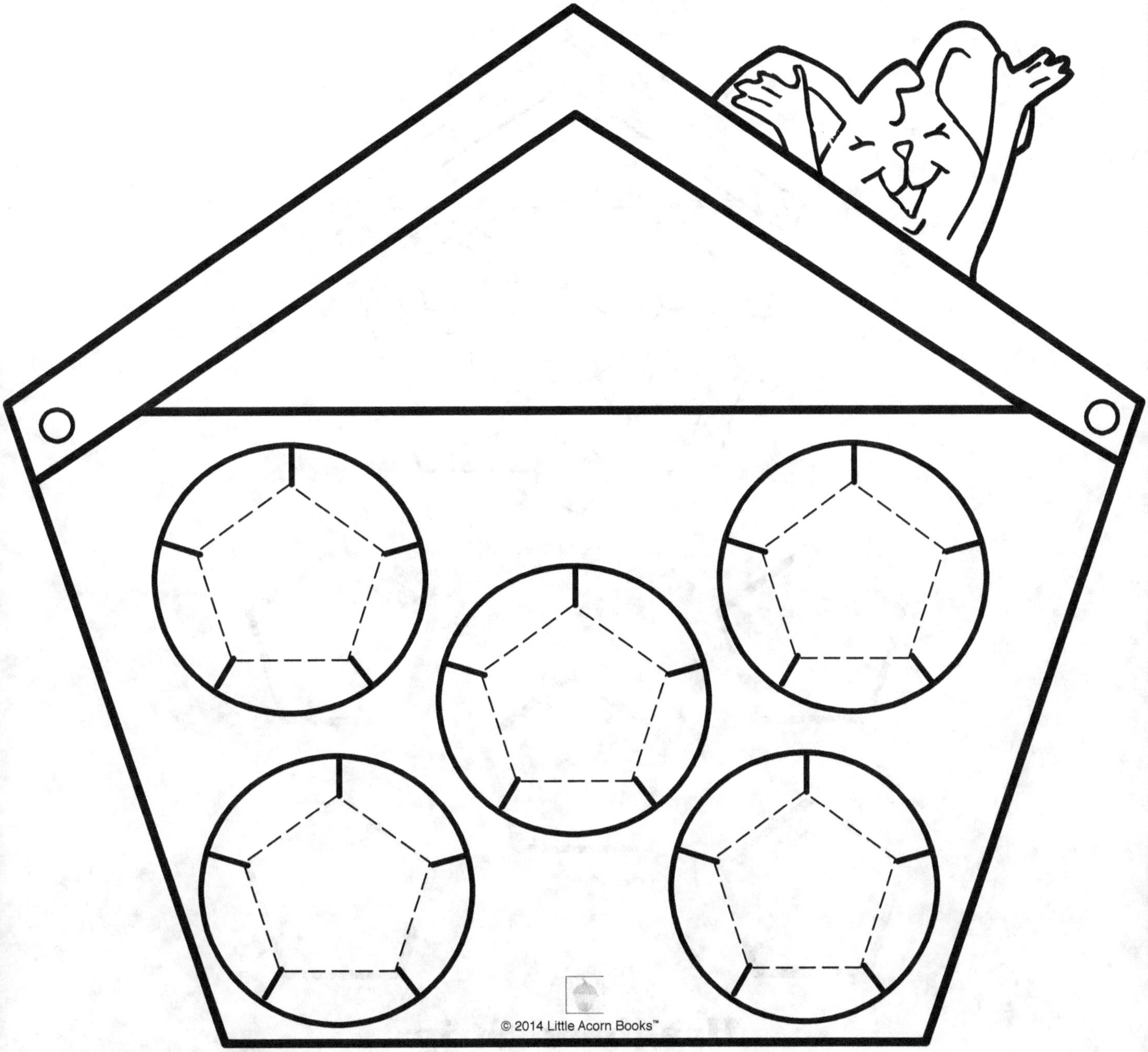

Shape Tag

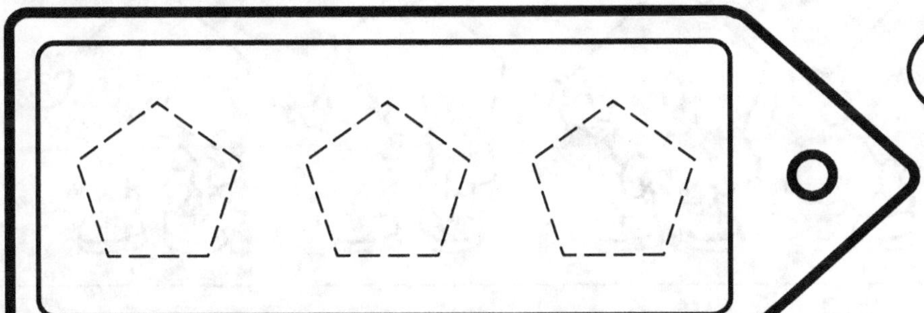

Trace the shapes.

© 2014 Little Acorn Books™

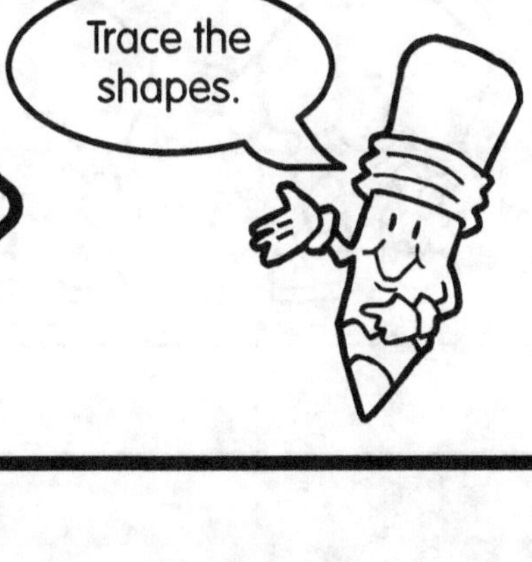

Pentagon Labels

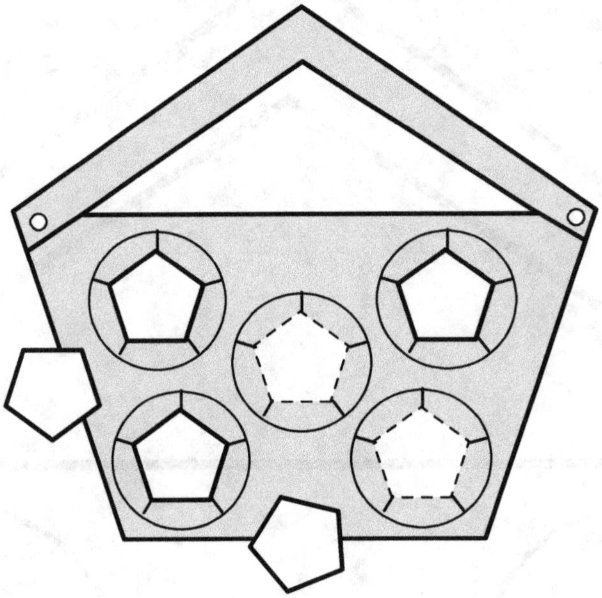

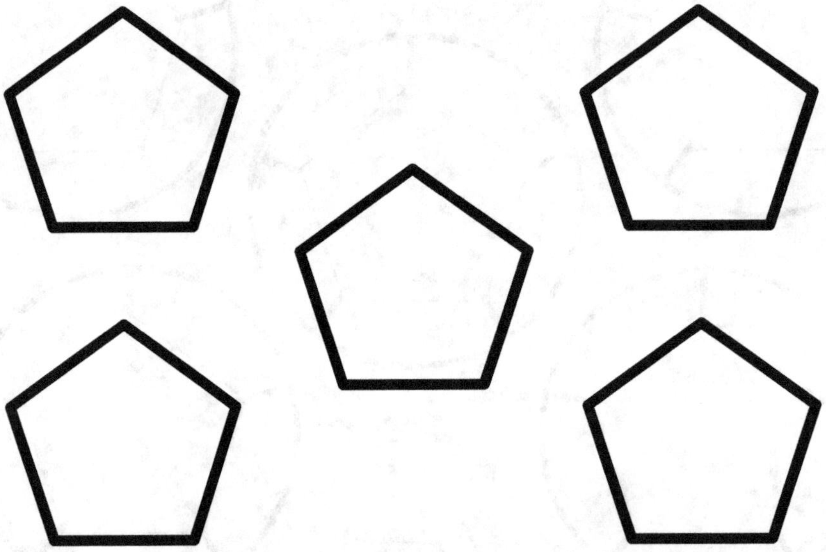

Headband Strip

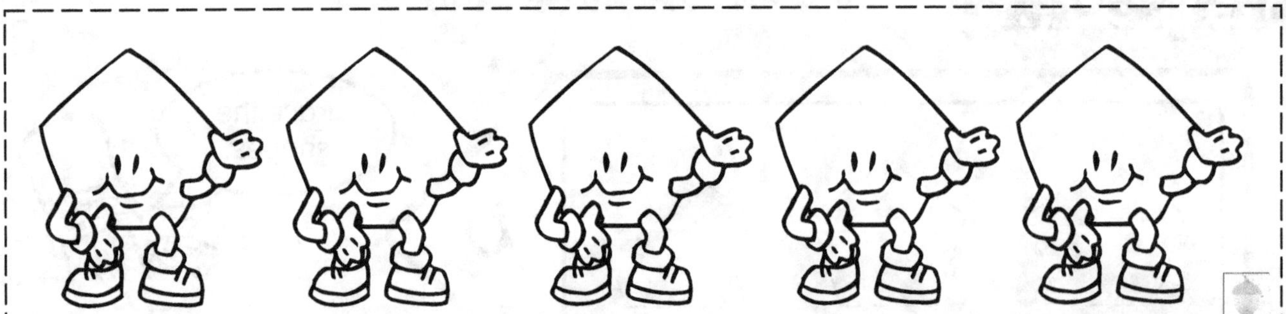

 LAB20147P • About Early Colors & Shapes • 978-1-937257-54-5 • © 2014 Little Acorn Books™

Honey Bee Hive

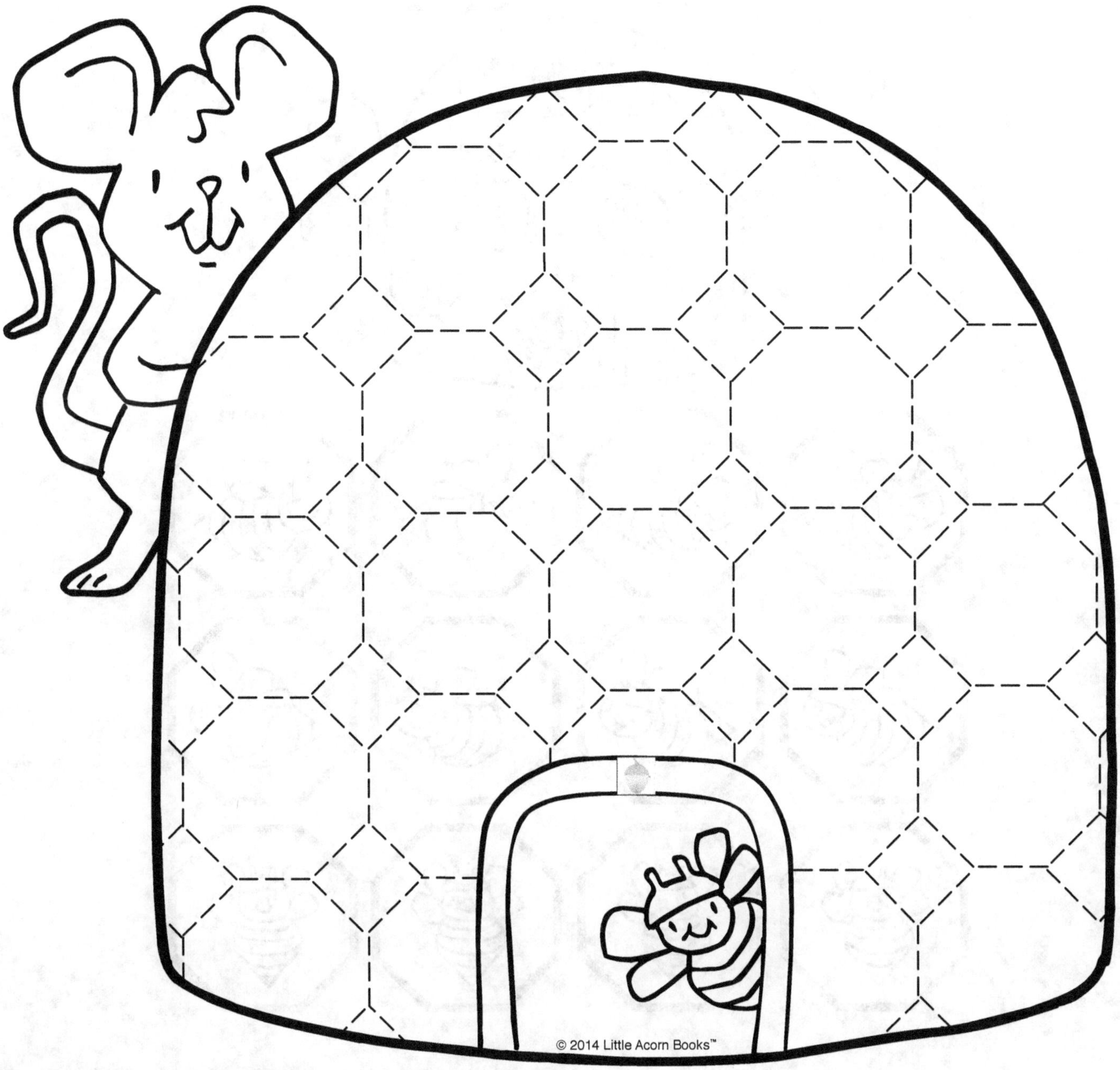

Shape Tag

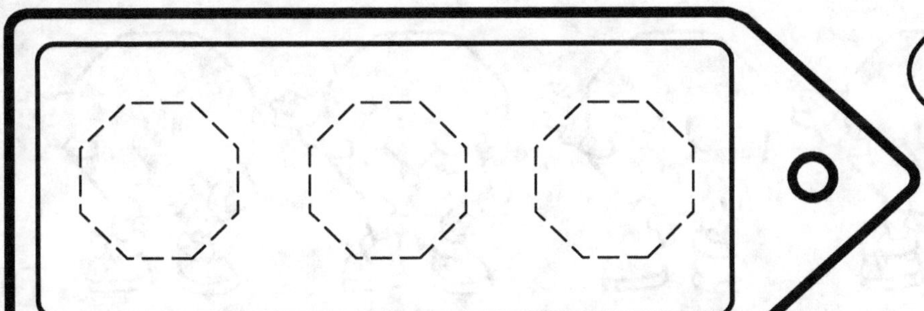

Trace the shapes.

© 2014 Little Acorn Books™

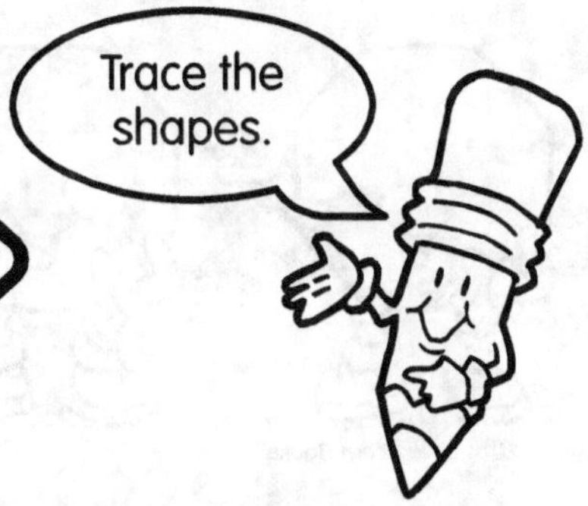

Octagon Tiles

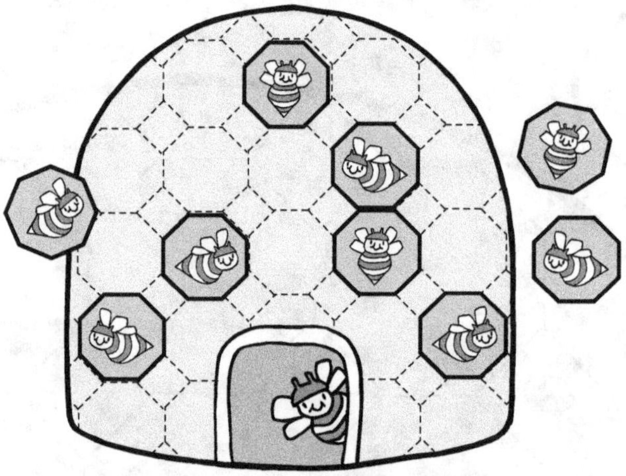

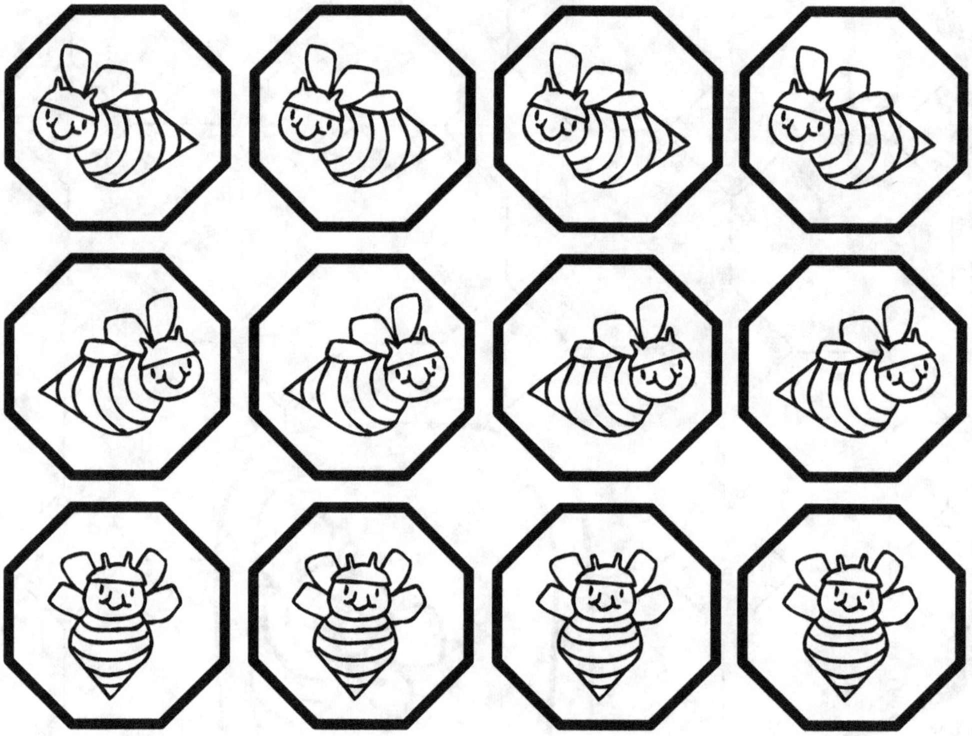

Headband Strip

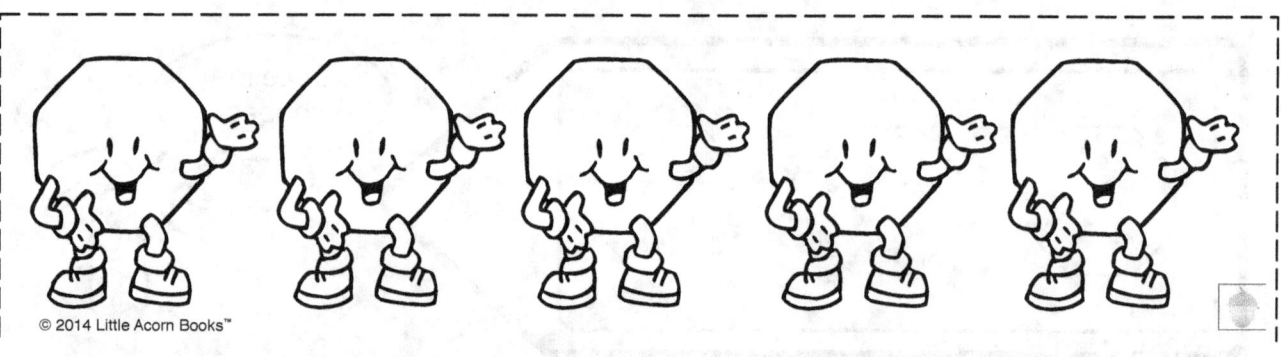

LAB20147P • About Early Colors & Shapes • 978-1-937257-54-5 • © 2014 Little Acorn Books™

Jeweled Crown

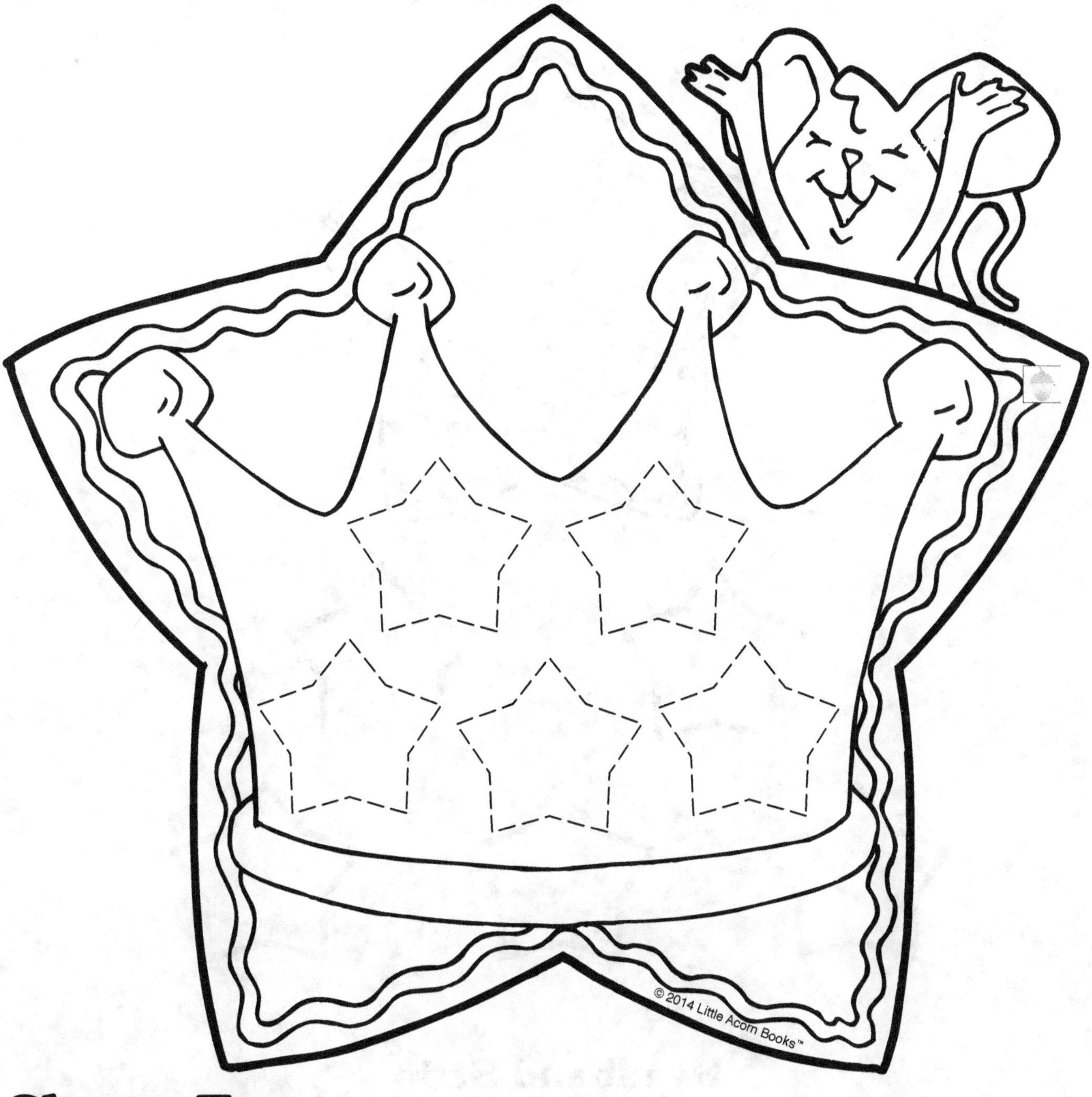

Shape Tag

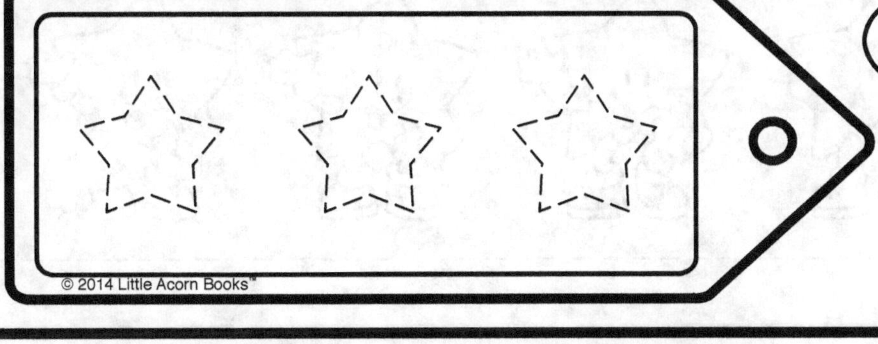

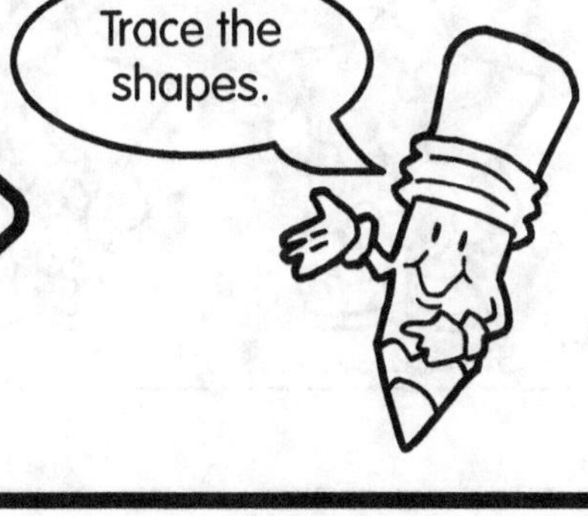

Trace the shapes.

Star Jewels

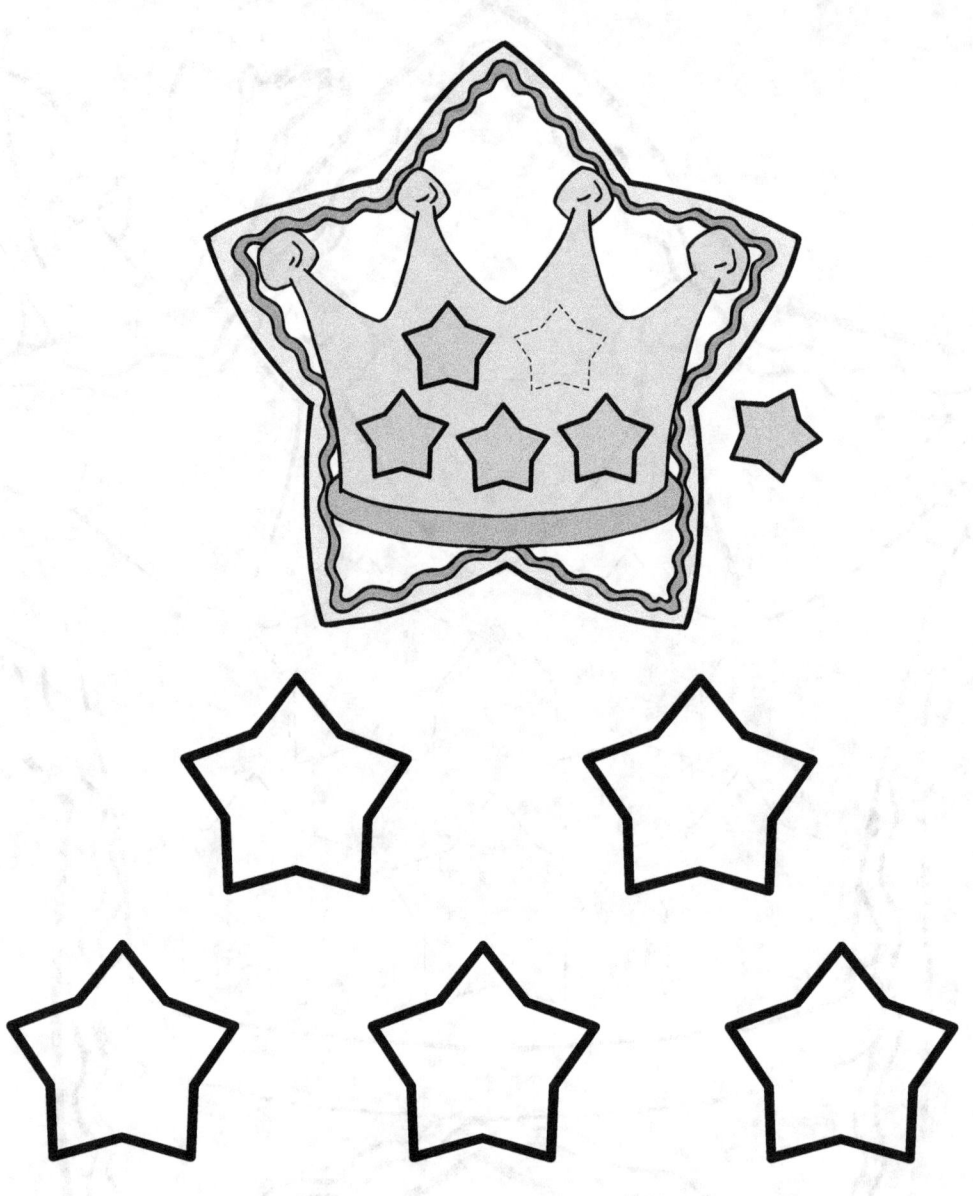

Headband Strip

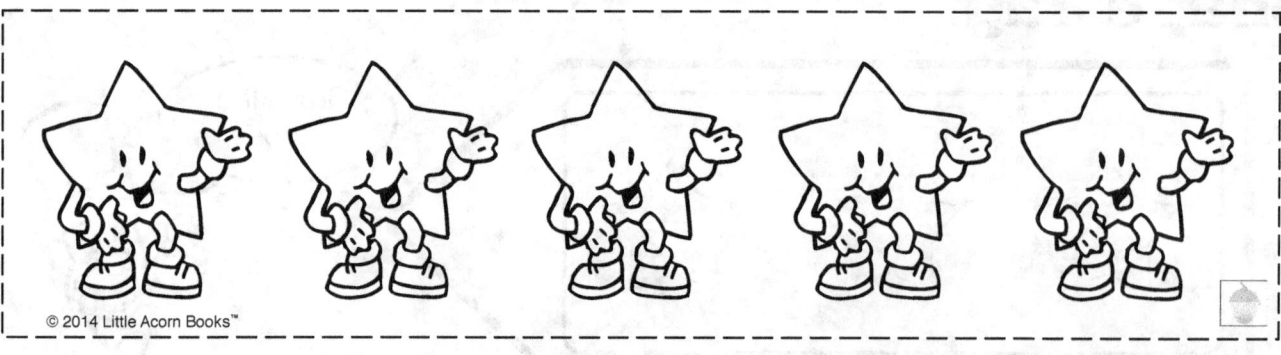

LAB20147P • About Early Colors & Shapes • 978-1-937257-54-5 • © 2014 Little Acorn Books™

Candy Box

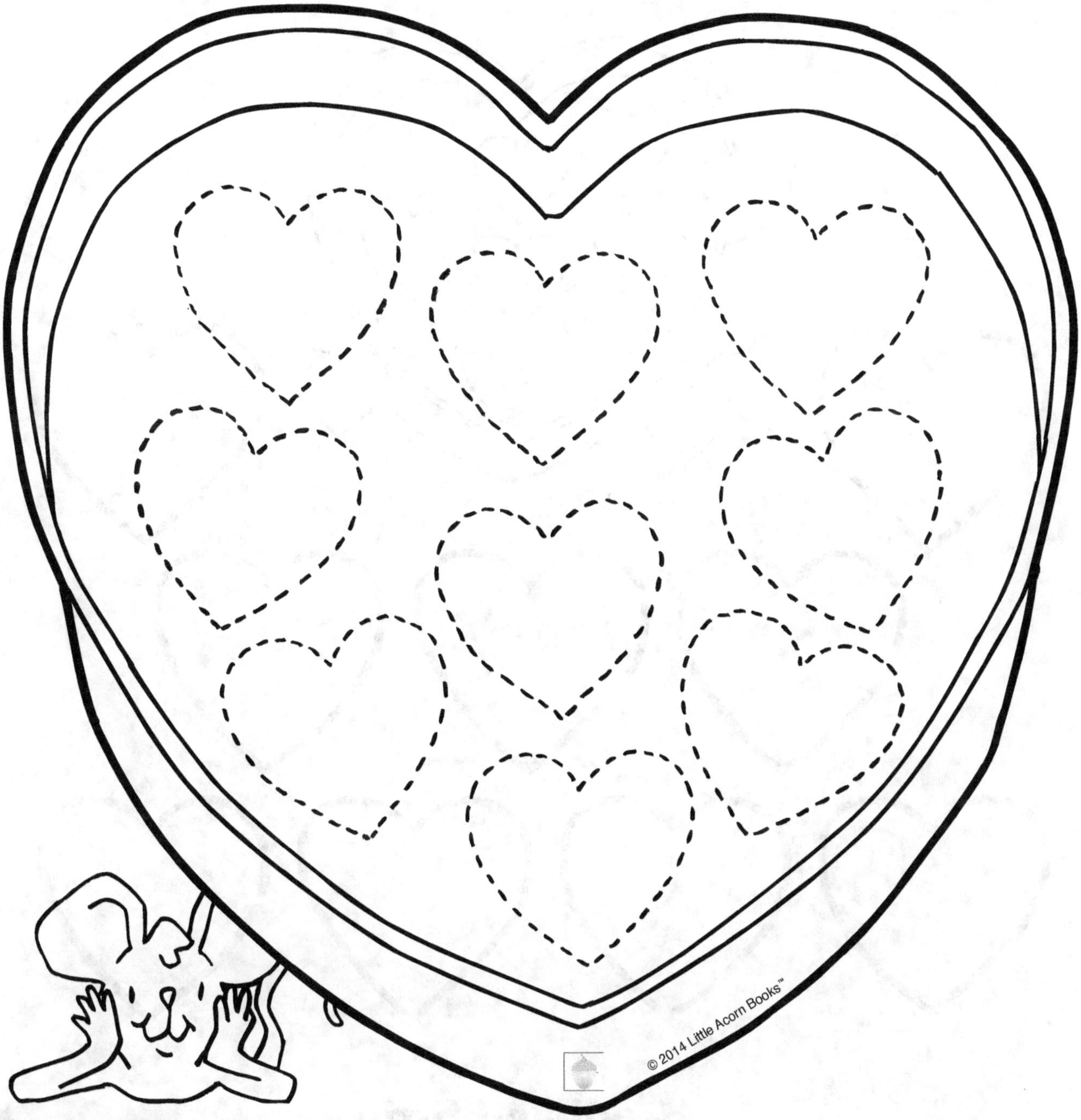

Shape Tag

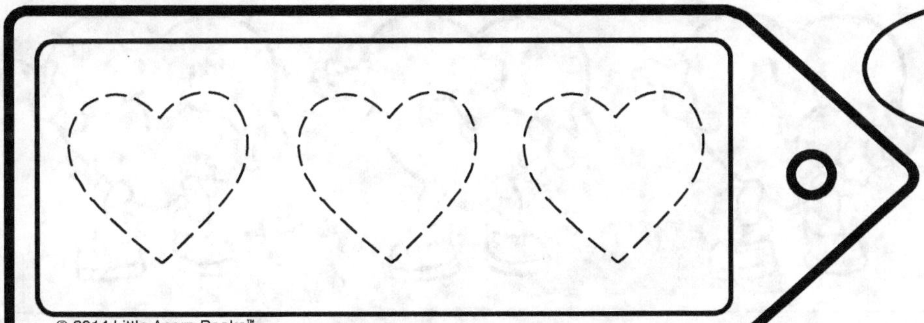

Trace the shapes.

© 2014 Little Acorn Books™

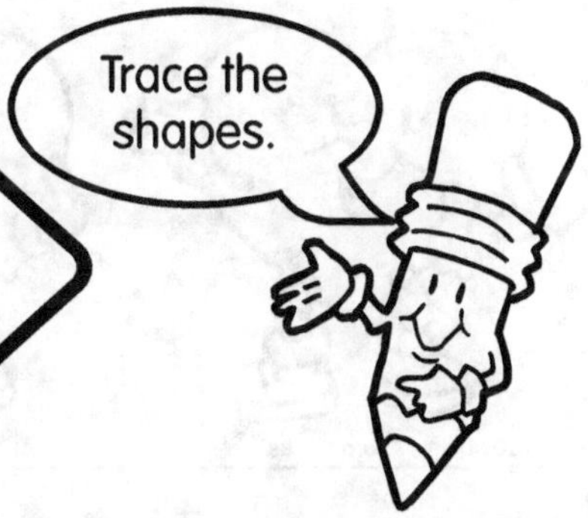

Heart Candy

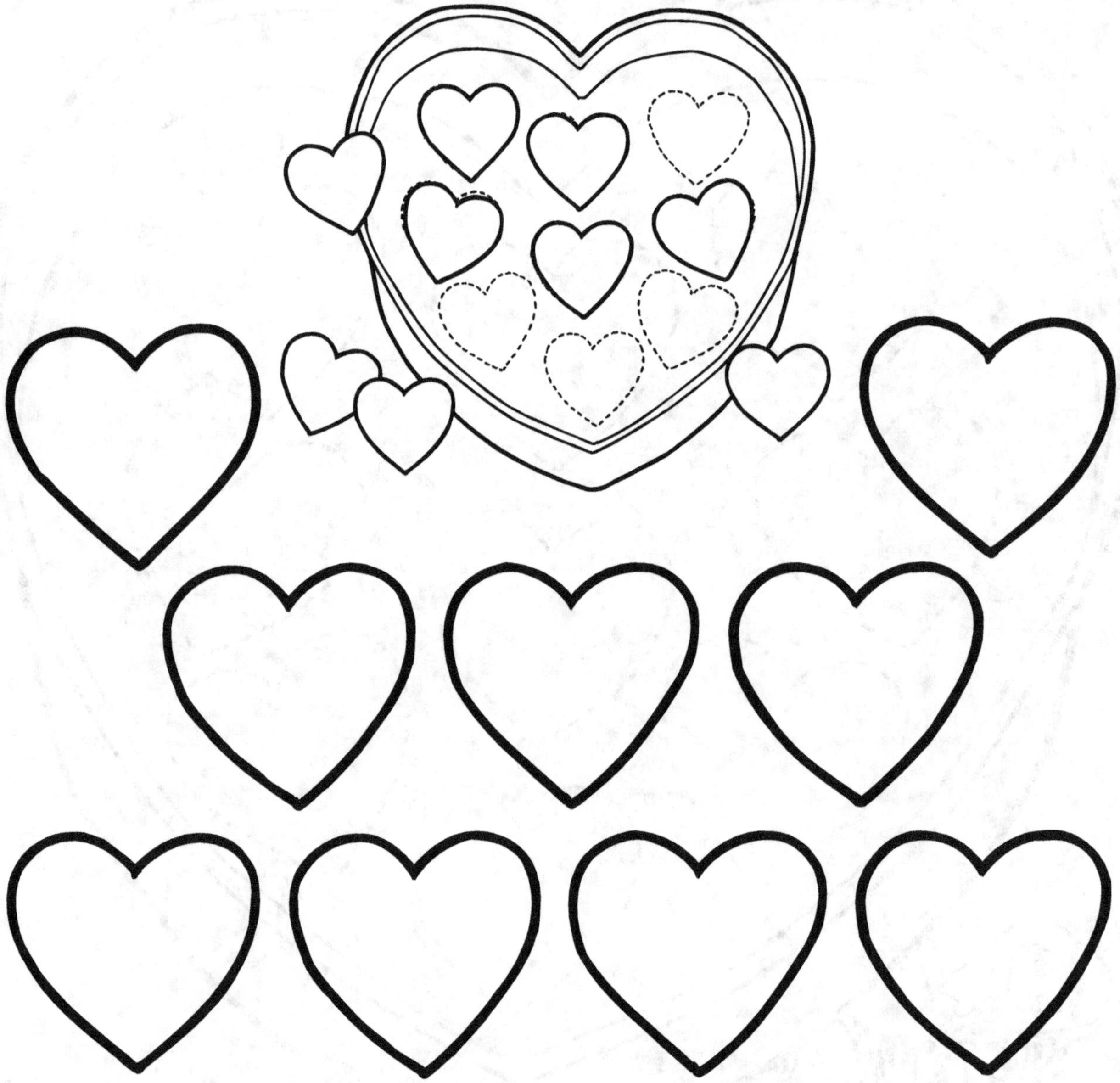

Headband Strip

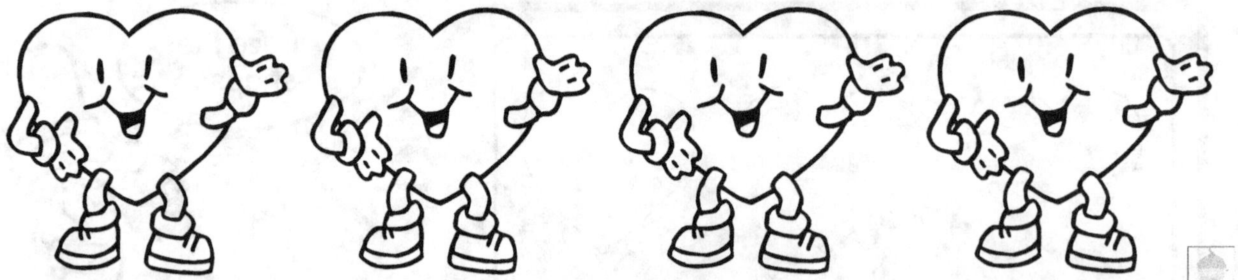

Match a Shape Treasure Chest

Reproduce and color the game board patterns and two sets of jewel shapes. Cut out and glue each game board pattern to the inside of a folder. Laminate the game board folder and jewel shapes. Cut out the jewel shapes. Tape an envelope to the back of the game board folder to store jewels. Option: Reproduce, color, and glue each page of game cards to the back of a sheet of gift wrap, then laminate and cut out the cards.

Treasure Chest Game Board

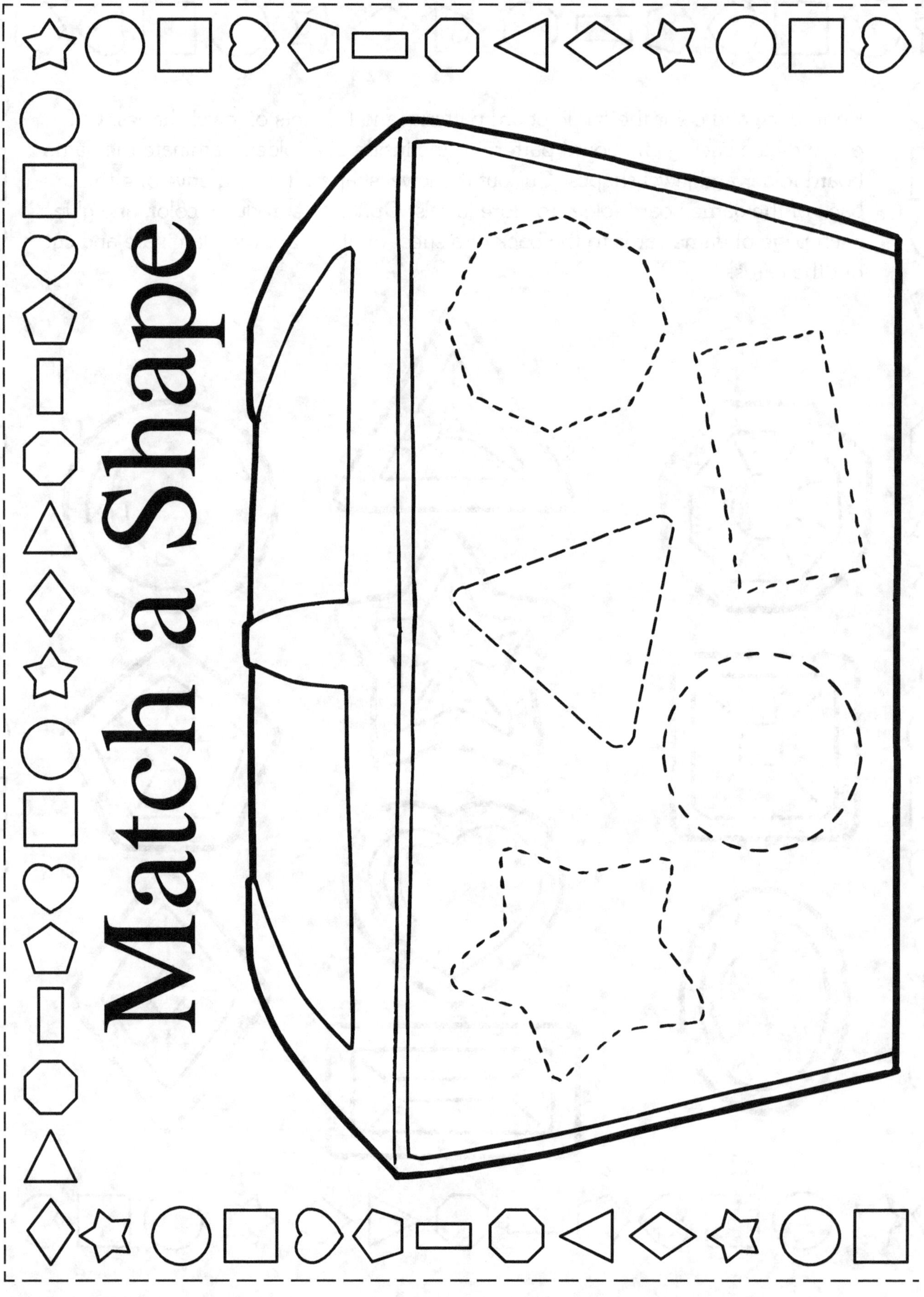

Match a Shape

LAB20147P • About Early Colors & Shapes • 978-1-937257-54-5 • © 2014 Little Acorn Books™

Treasure Chest Game Board

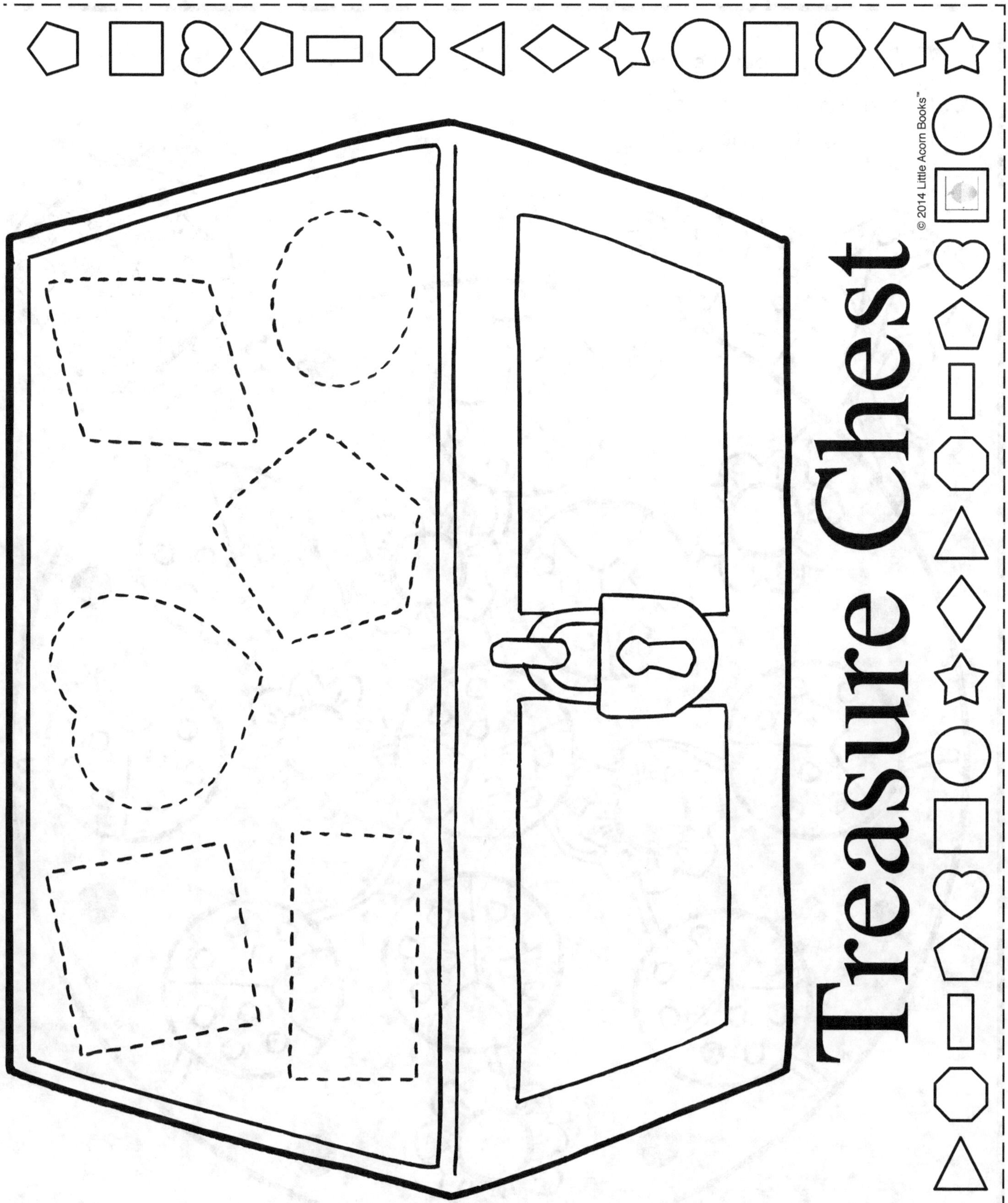

Circle Lacing Card

1. Color and cut out the circle.
2. Punch a hole at each dot.
3. Lace yarn through each hole.

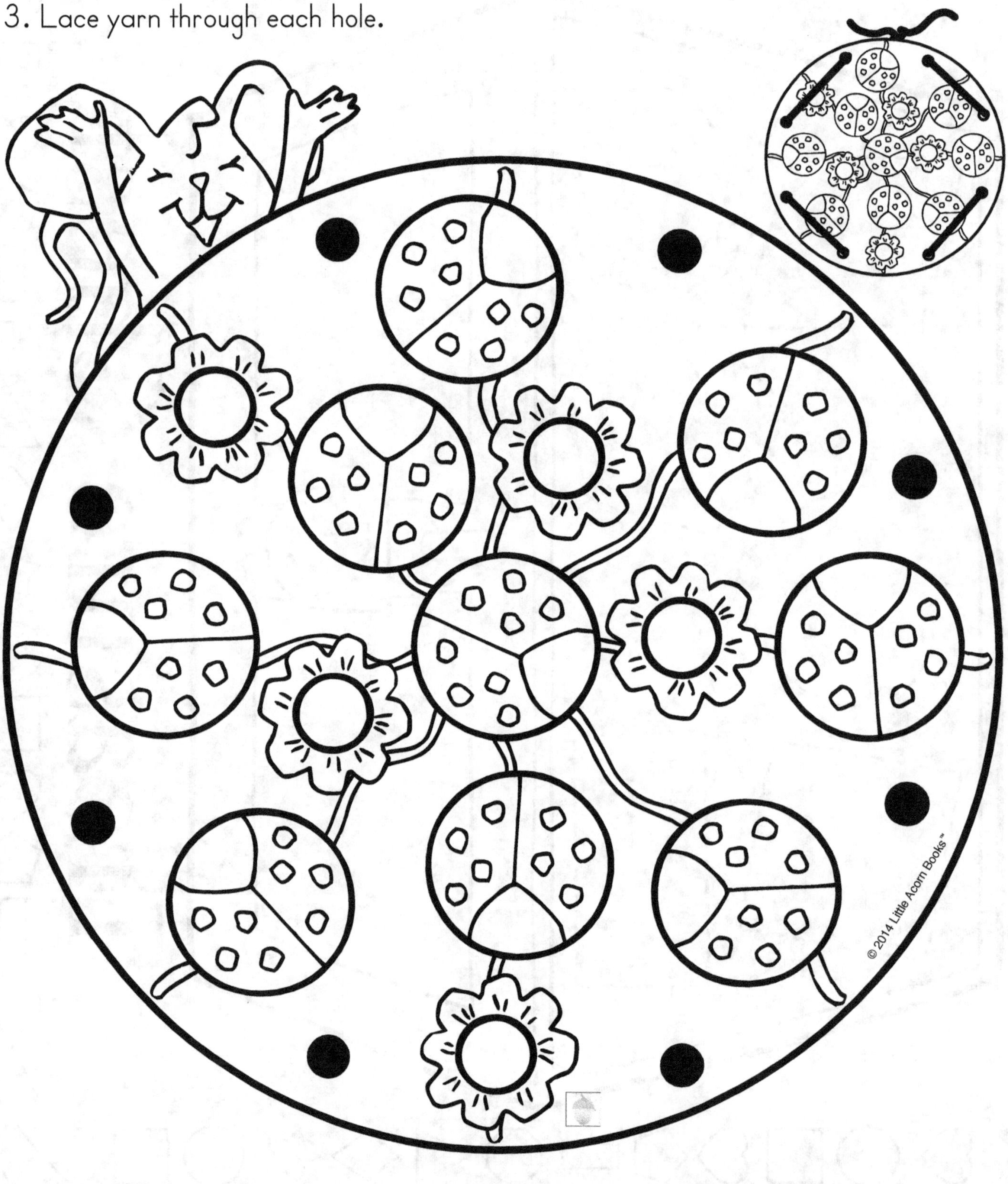

© 2014 Little Acorn Books™

 LAB20147P • About Early Colors & Shapes • 978-1-937257-54-5 • © 2014 Little Acorn Books™

Square Lacing Card

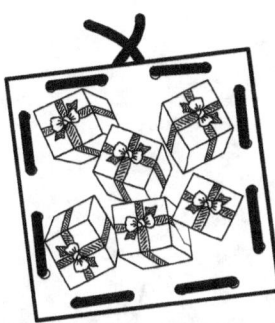

1. Color and cut out the square.
2. Punch a hole at each dot.
3. Lace yarn through each hole.

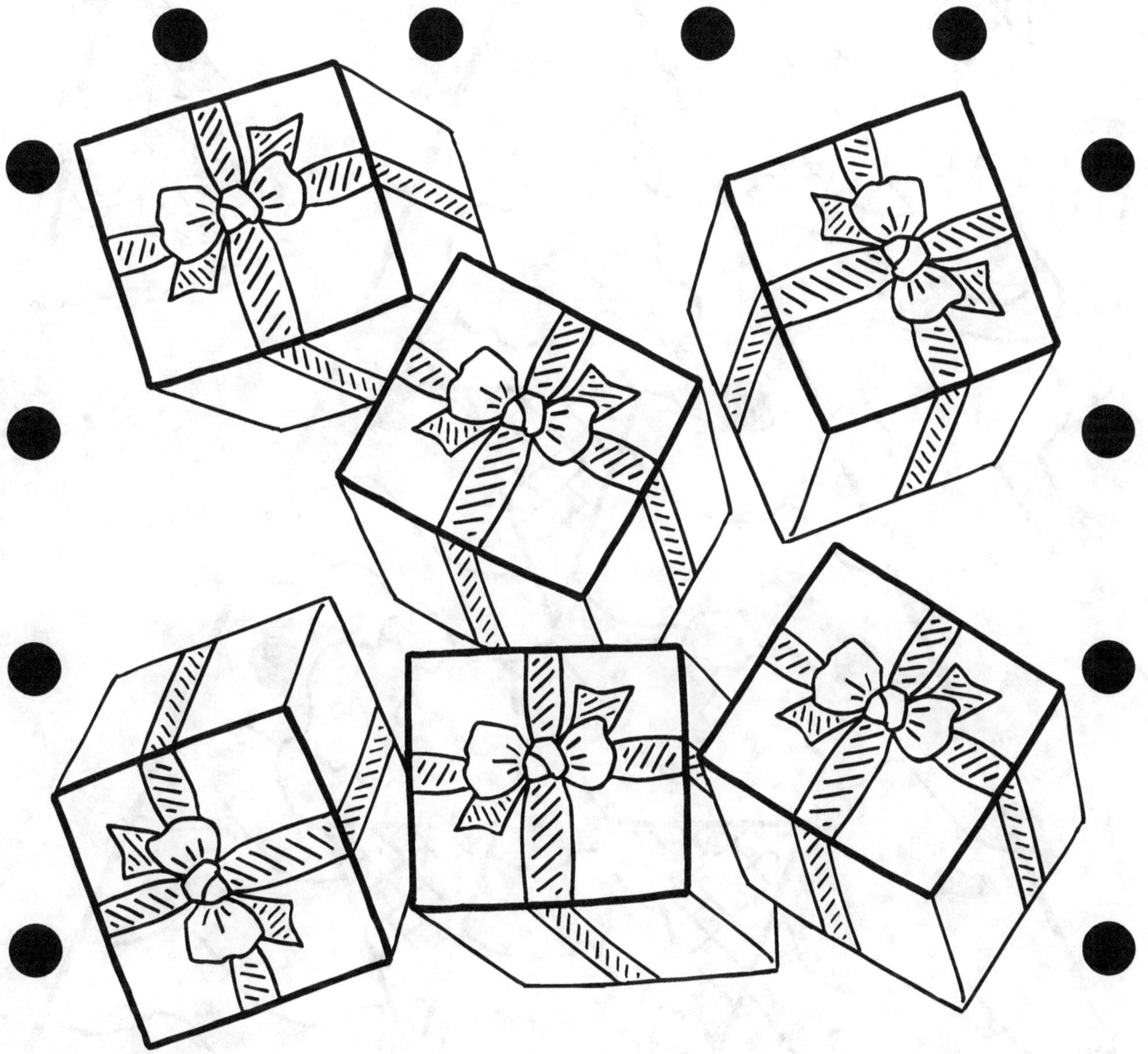

Triangle Lacing Card

1. Color and cut out the triangle.
2. Punch a hole at each dot.
3. Lace yarn through each hole.

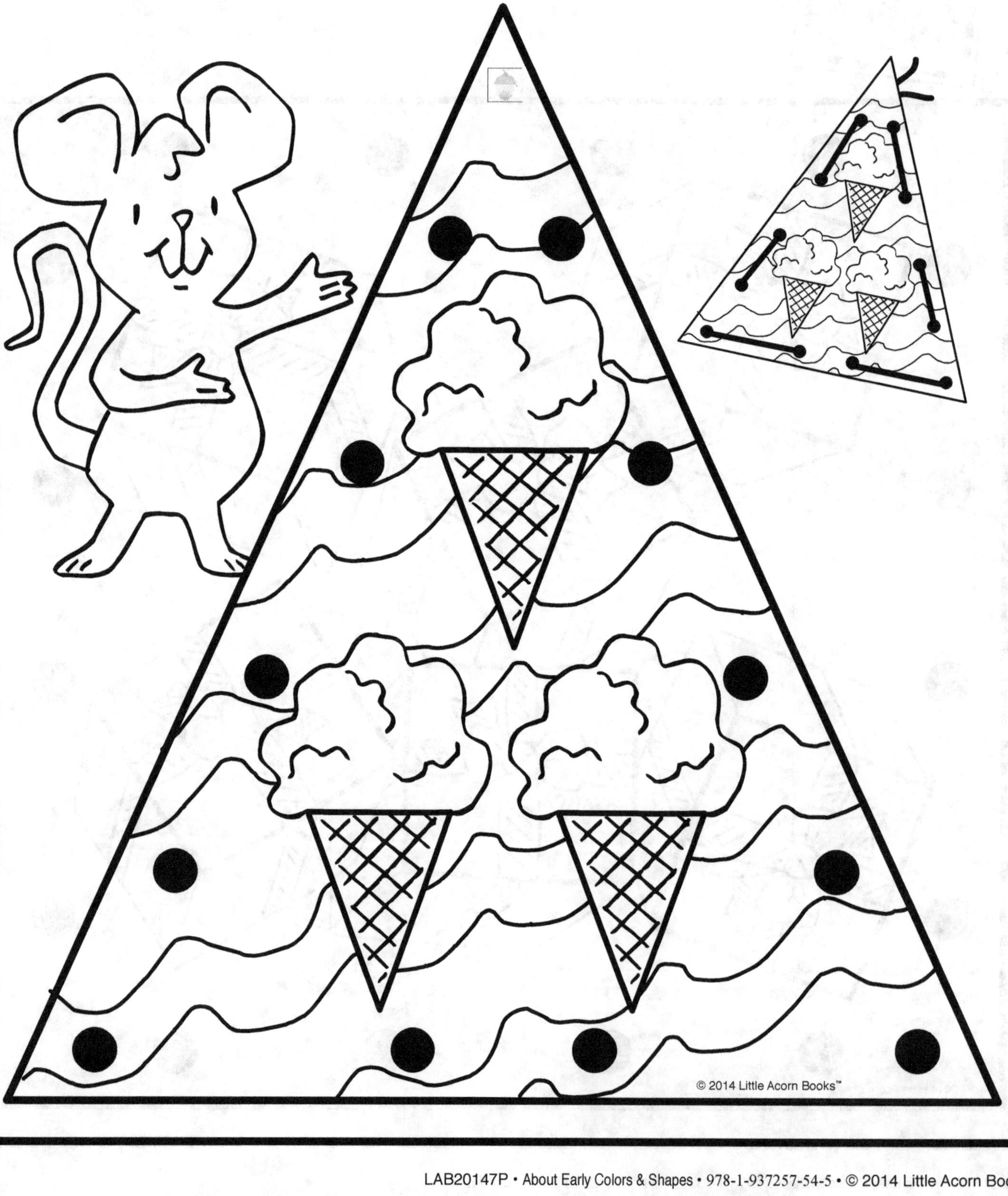

LAB20147P • About Early Colors & Shapes • 978-1-937257-54-5 • © 2014 Little Acorn Books™

© 2014 Little Acorn Books™

Rectangle Lacing Card

1. Color and cut out the rectangle.
2. Punch a hole at each dot.
3. Lace yarn through each hole.

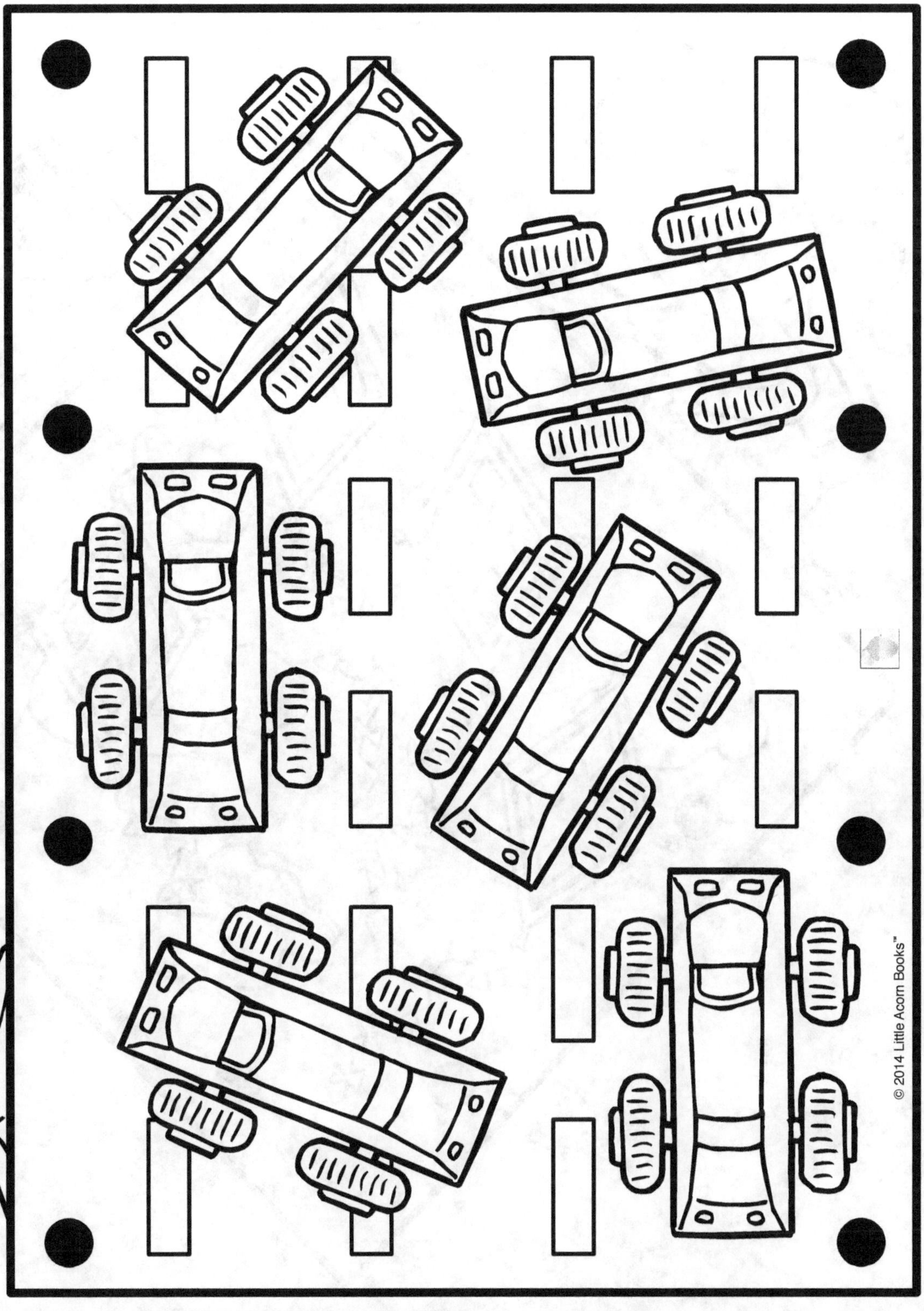

© 2014 Little Acorn Books™

Diamond Lacing Card

1. Color and cut out the diamond.
2. Punch a hole at each dot.
3. Lace yarn through each hole.

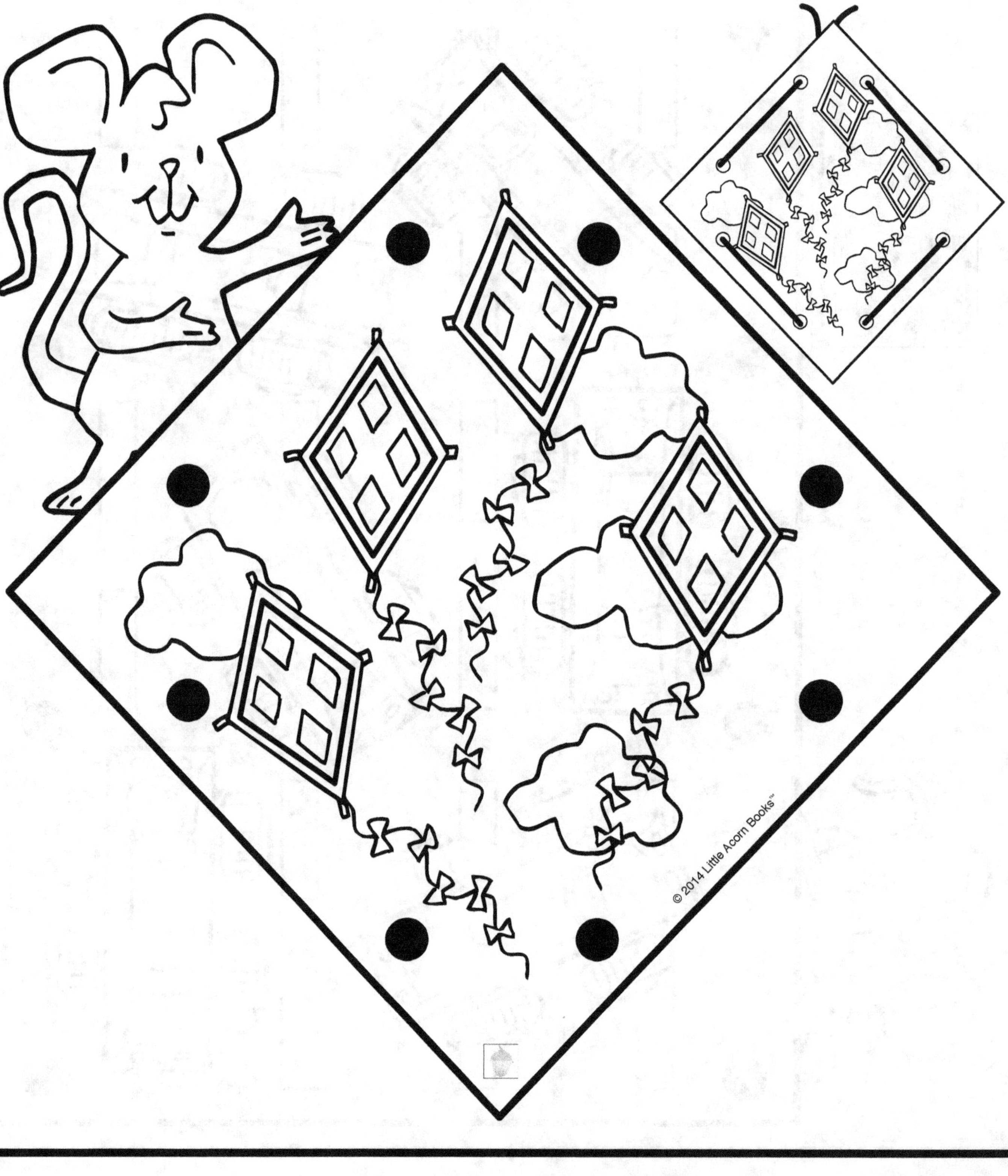

© 2014 Little Acorn Books™

 LAB20147P • About Early Colors & Shapes • 978-1-937257-54-5 • © 2014 Little Acorn Books™

Oval Lacing Card

1. Color and cut out the oval.
2. Punch a hole at each dot.
3. Lace yarn through each hole.

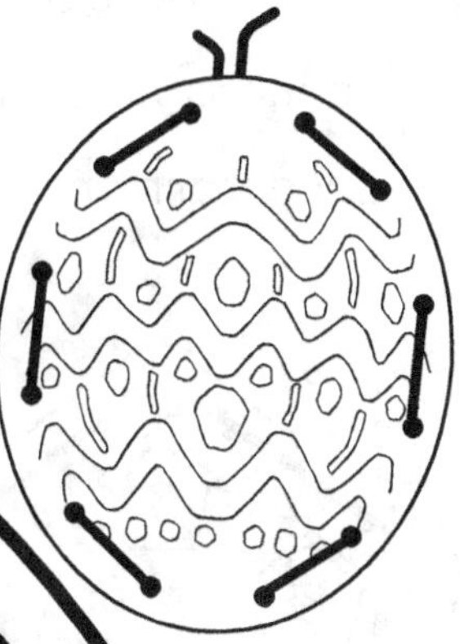

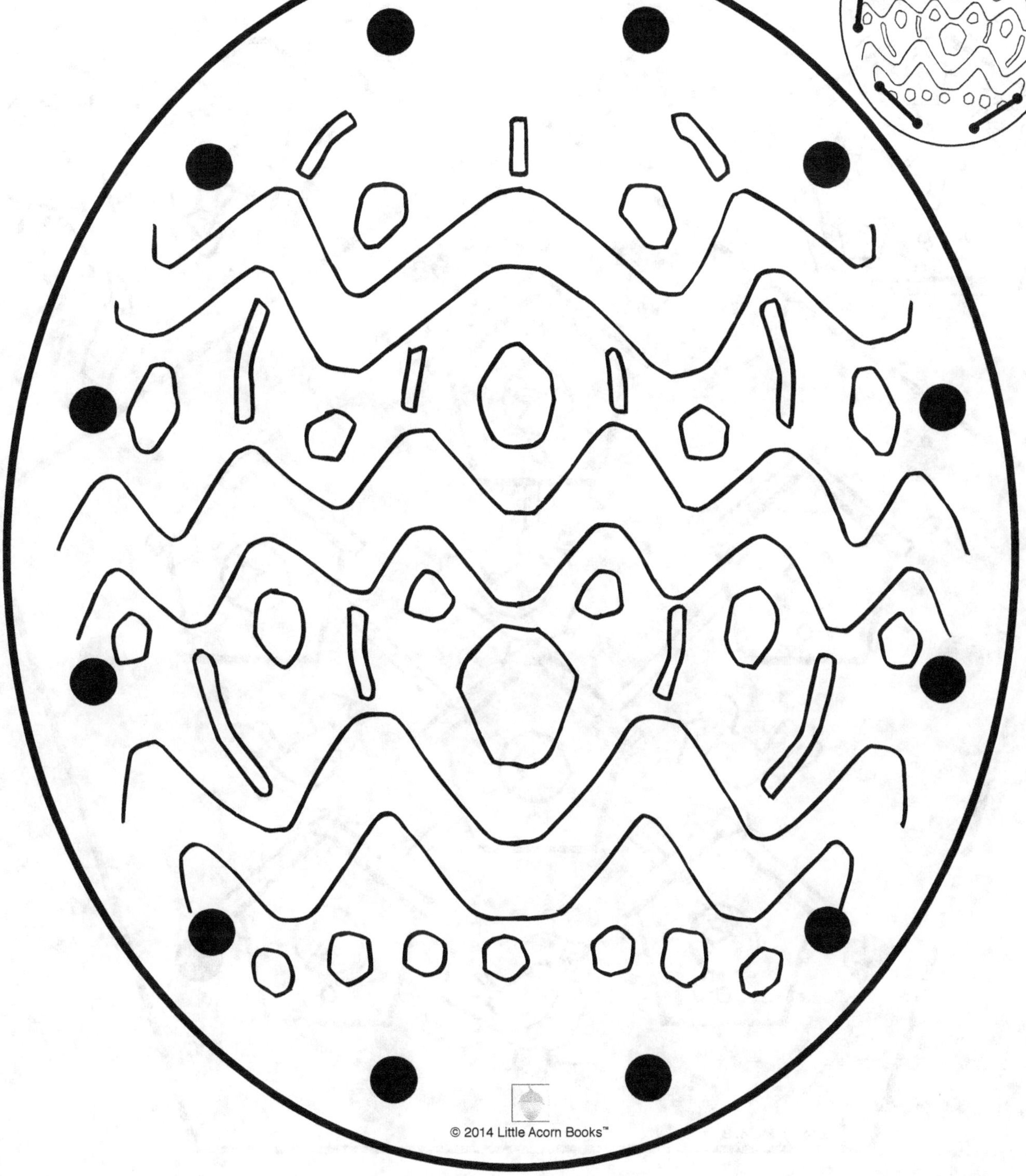

Pentagon Lacing Card

1. Color and cut out the pentagon.
2. Punch a hole at each dot.
3. Lace yarn through each hole.

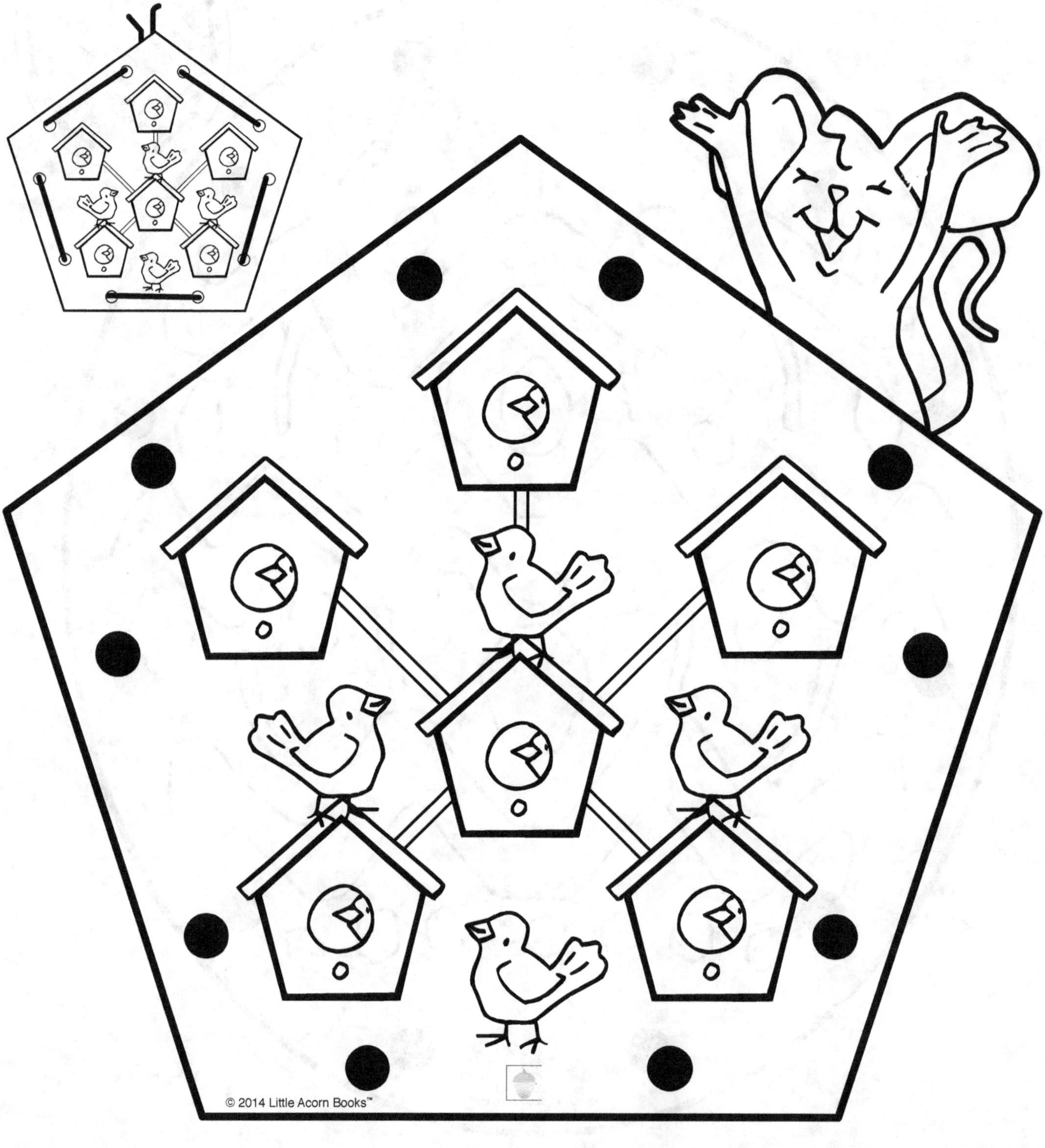

 LAB20147P • About Early Colors & Shapes • 978-1-937257-54-5 • © 2014 Little Acorn Books™

Octagon Lacing Card

1. Color and cut out the octagon.
2. Punch a hole at each dot.
3. Lace yarn through each hole.

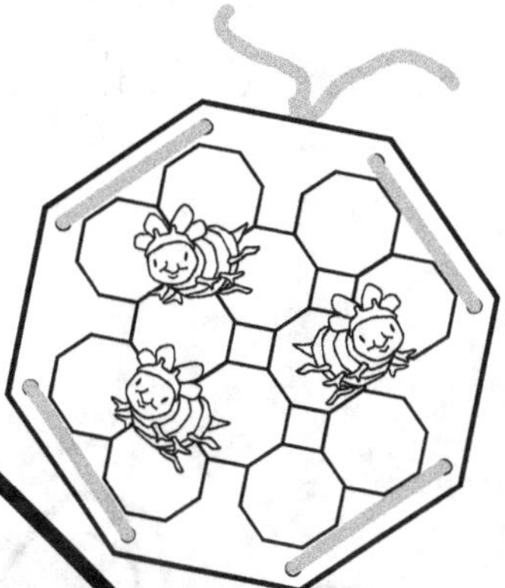

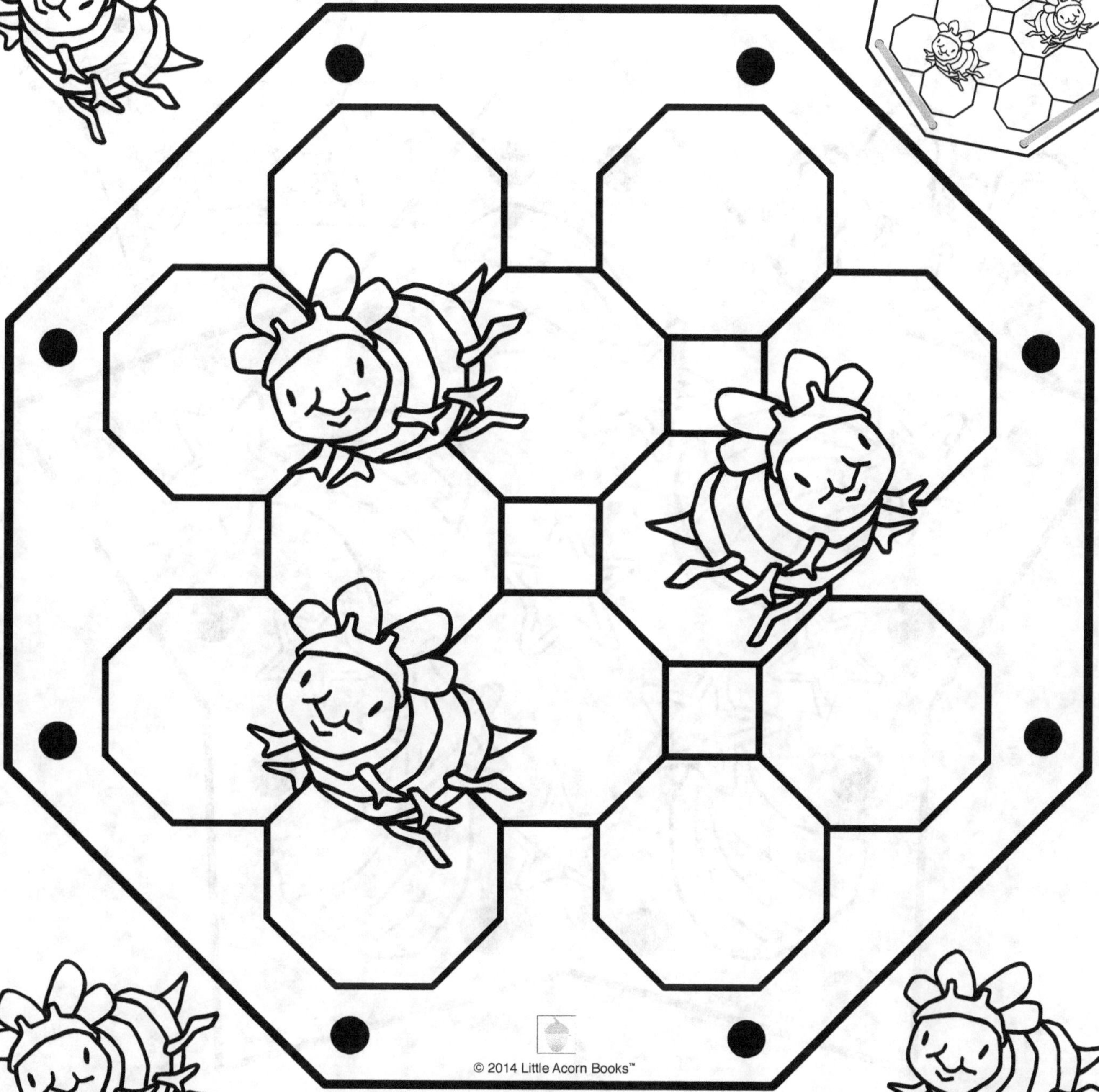

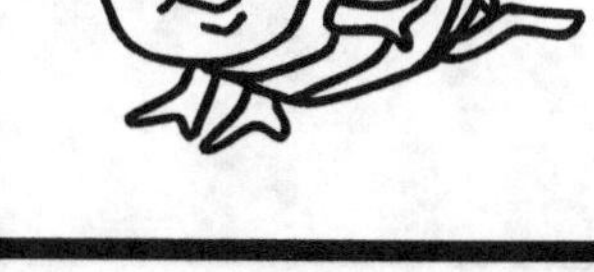

Star Lacing Card

1. Color and cut out the star.
2. Punch a hole at each dot.
3. Lace yarn through each hole.

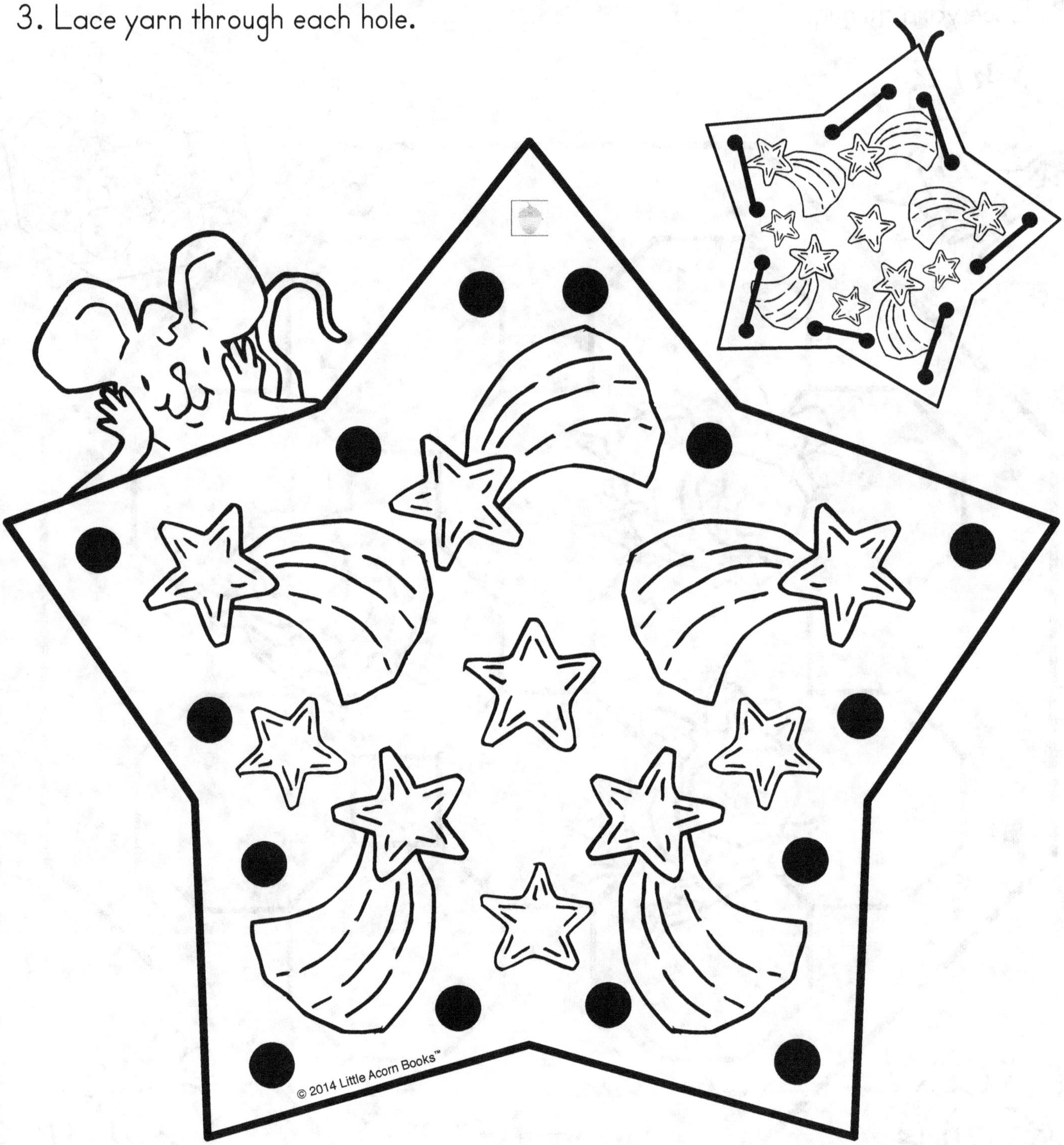

 LAB20147P • About Early Colors & Shapes • 978-1-937257-54-5 • © 2014 Little Acorn Books™

Heart Lacing Card

1. Color and cut out the heart.
2. Punch a hole at each dot.
3. Lace yarn through each hole.

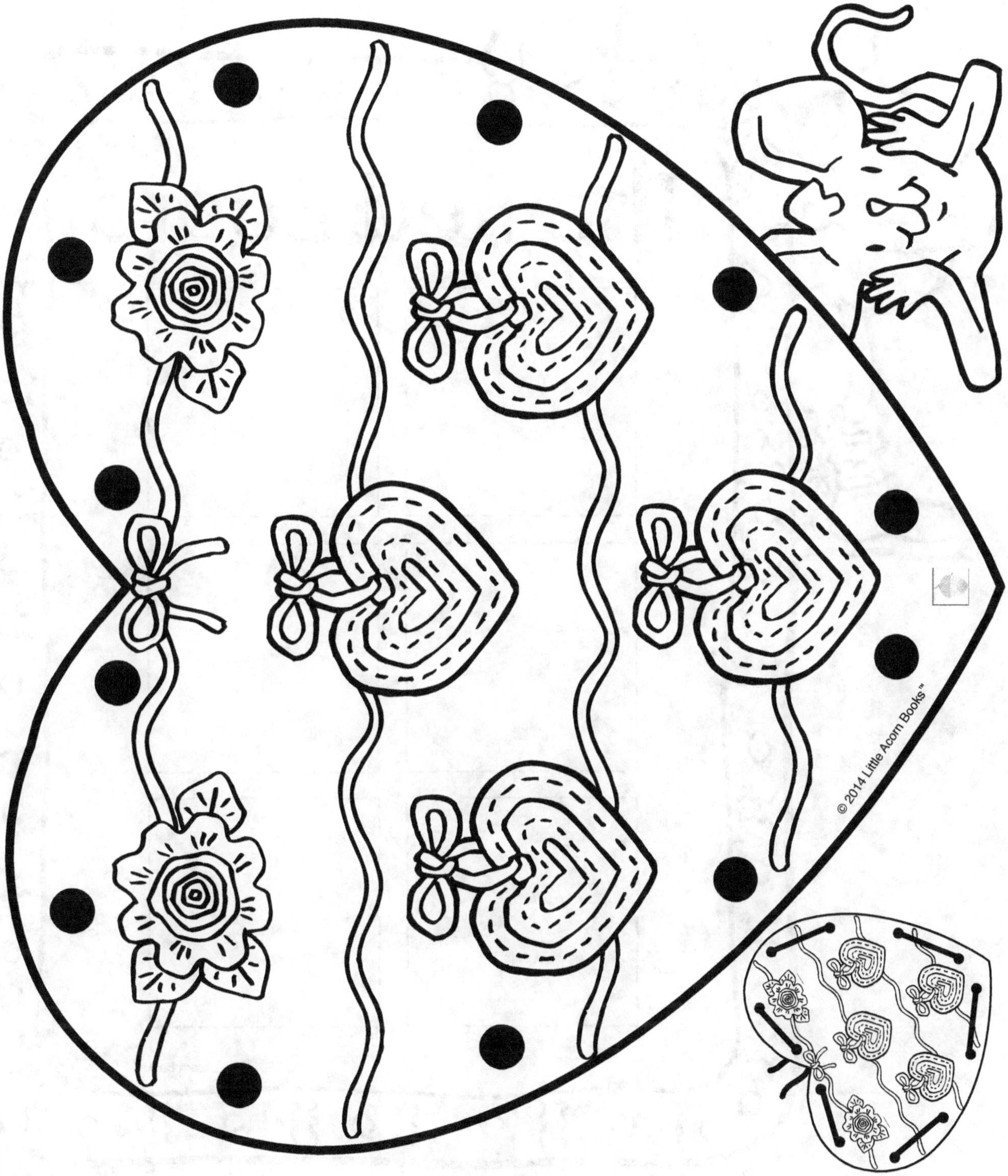

The Red Board

- Color, cut out and glue a **red** Color Board Cutout on each square.
- Color each square **red**.
- Cut out and glue **red** pictures on the squares.

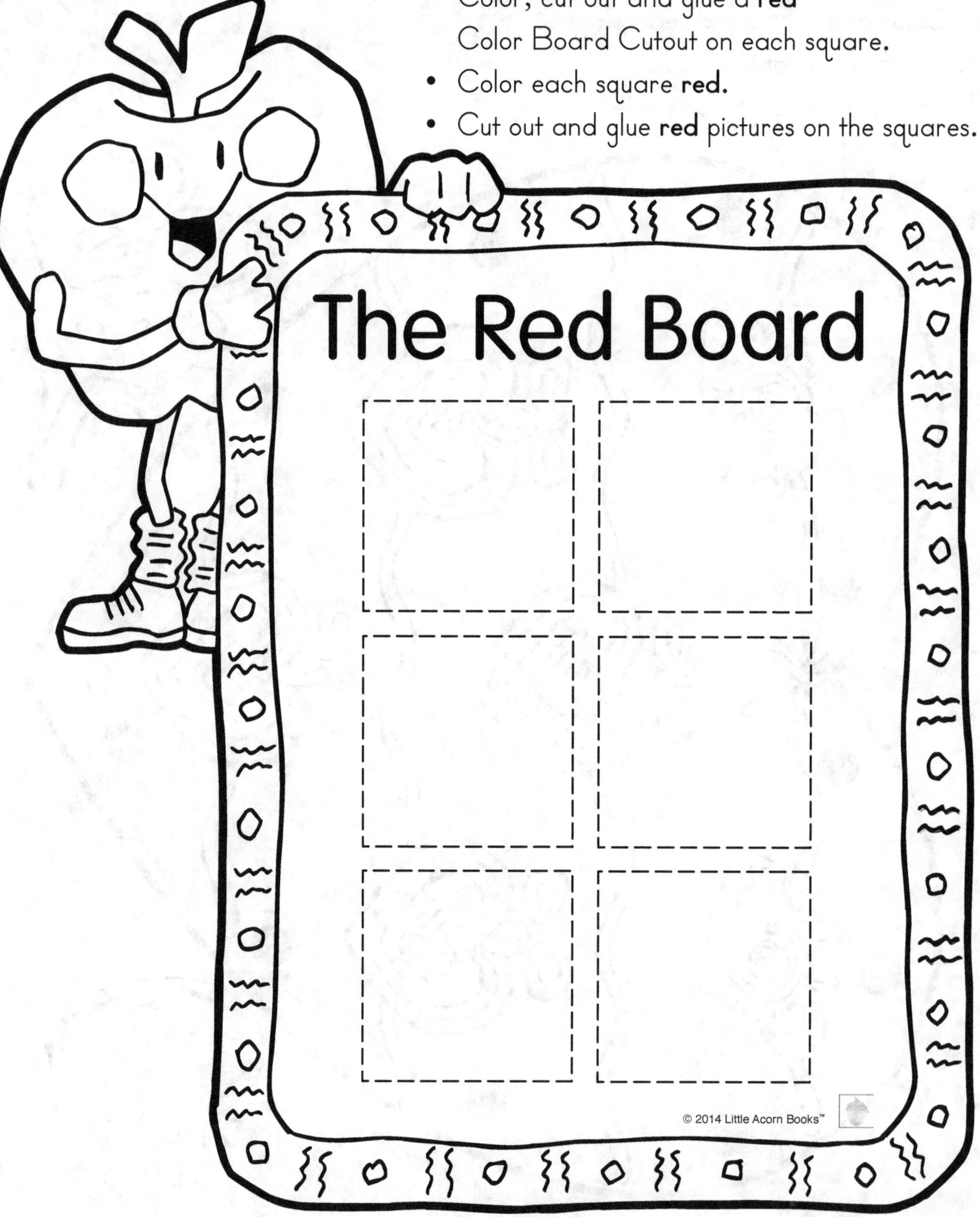

The Red Board

© 2014 Little Acorn Books™

LAB20147P • About Early Colors & Shapes • 978-1-937257-54-5 • © 2014 Little Acorn Books™

The Blue Board

- Color, cut out and glue a **blue** Color Board Cutout on each square.
- Color each square **blue.**
- Cut out and glue **blue** pictures on the squares.

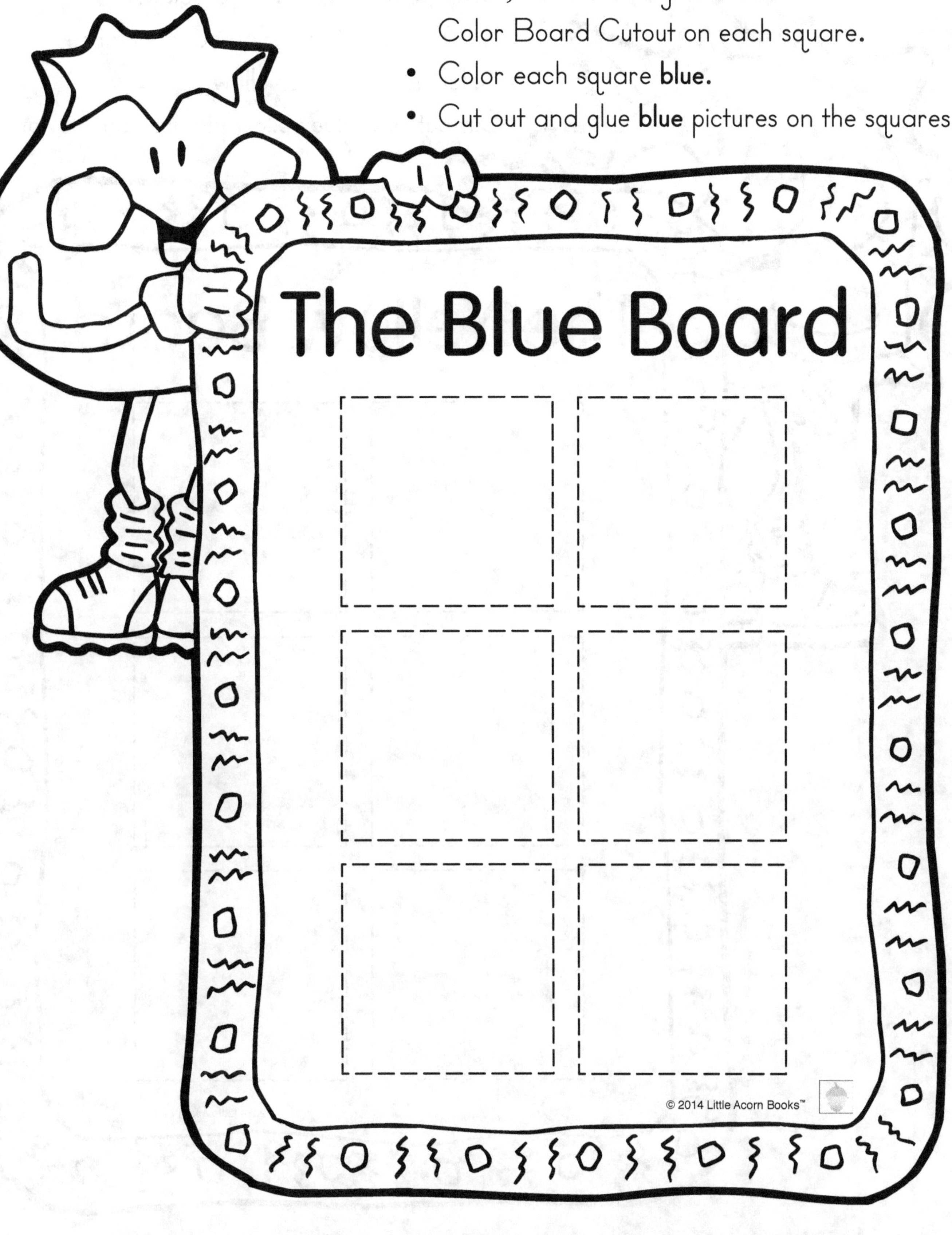

The Blue Board

© 2014 Little Acorn Books™

The Yellow Board

- Color, cut out and glue a **yellow** Color Board Cutout on each square.
- Color each square **yellow**.
- Cut out and glue **yellow** pictures on the squares.

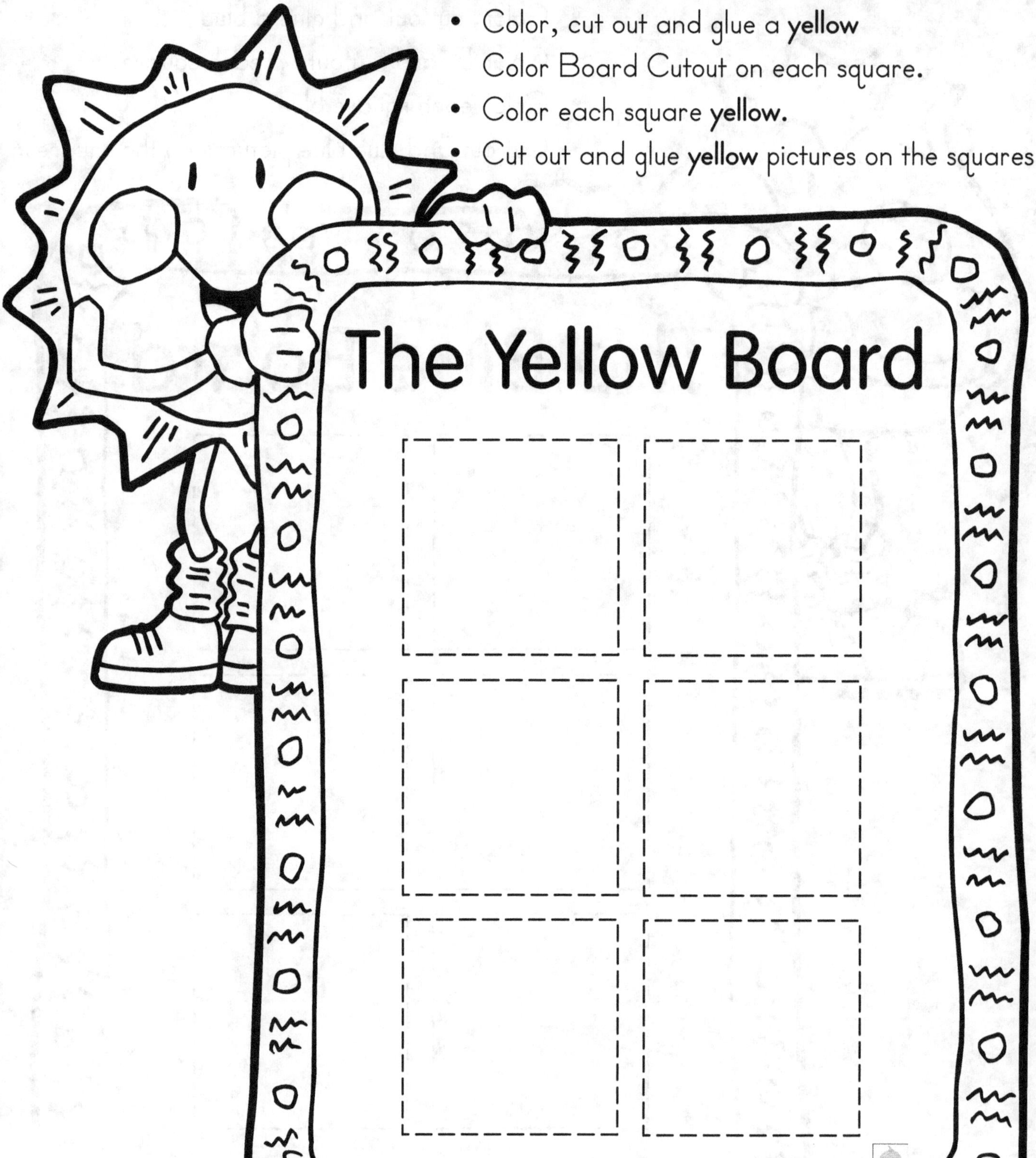

The Yellow Board

© 2014 Little Acorn Books™

LAB20147P • About Early Colors & Shapes • 978-1-937257-54-5 • © 2014 Little Acorn Books™

The Purple Board

- Color, cut out and glue a **purple** Color Board Cutout on each square.
- Color each square **purple**.
- Cut out and glue **purple** pictures on the squares.

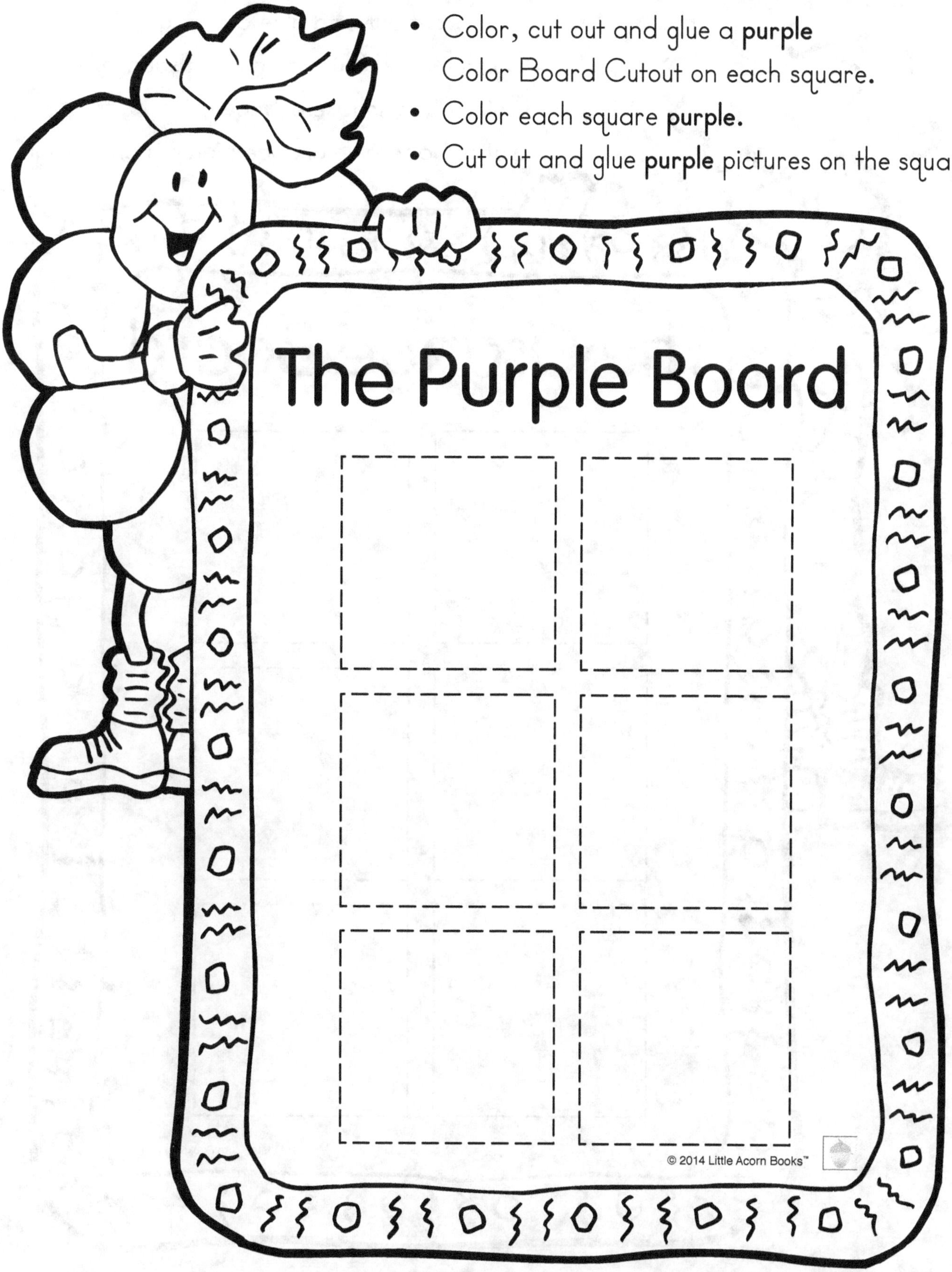

The Purple Board

© 2014 Little Acorn Books™

The Orange Board

- Color, cut out and glue a **orange** Color Board Cutout on each square.
- Color each square **orange**.
- Cut out and glue **orange** pictures on the squares.

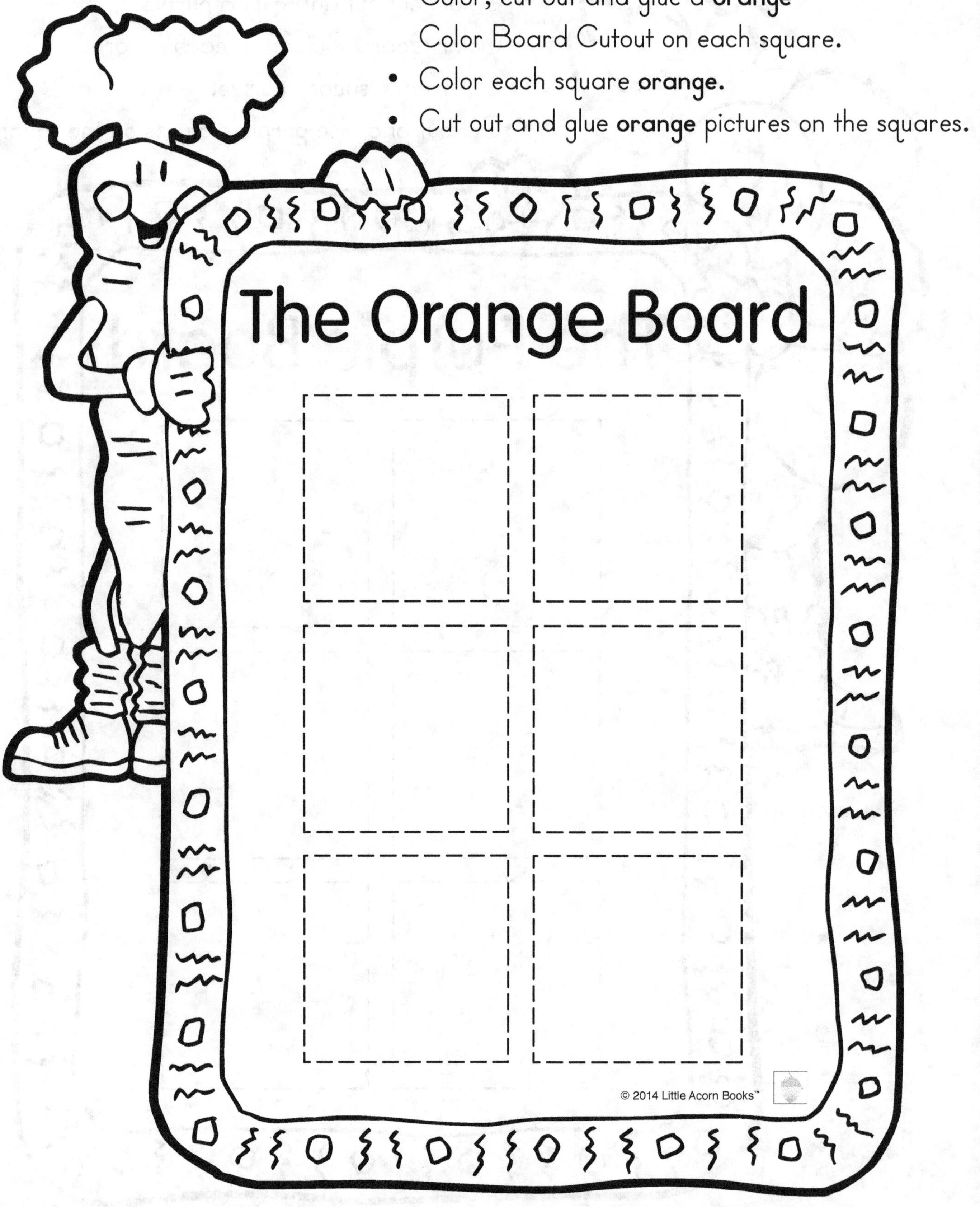

The Orange Board

© 2014 Little Acorn Books™

 LAB20147P • About Early Colors & Shapes • 978-1-937257-54-5 • © 2014 Little Acorn Books™

The Brown Board

- Color, cut out and glue a **brown** Color Board Cutout on each square.
- Color each square **brown**.
- Cut out and glue **brown** pictures on the squares.

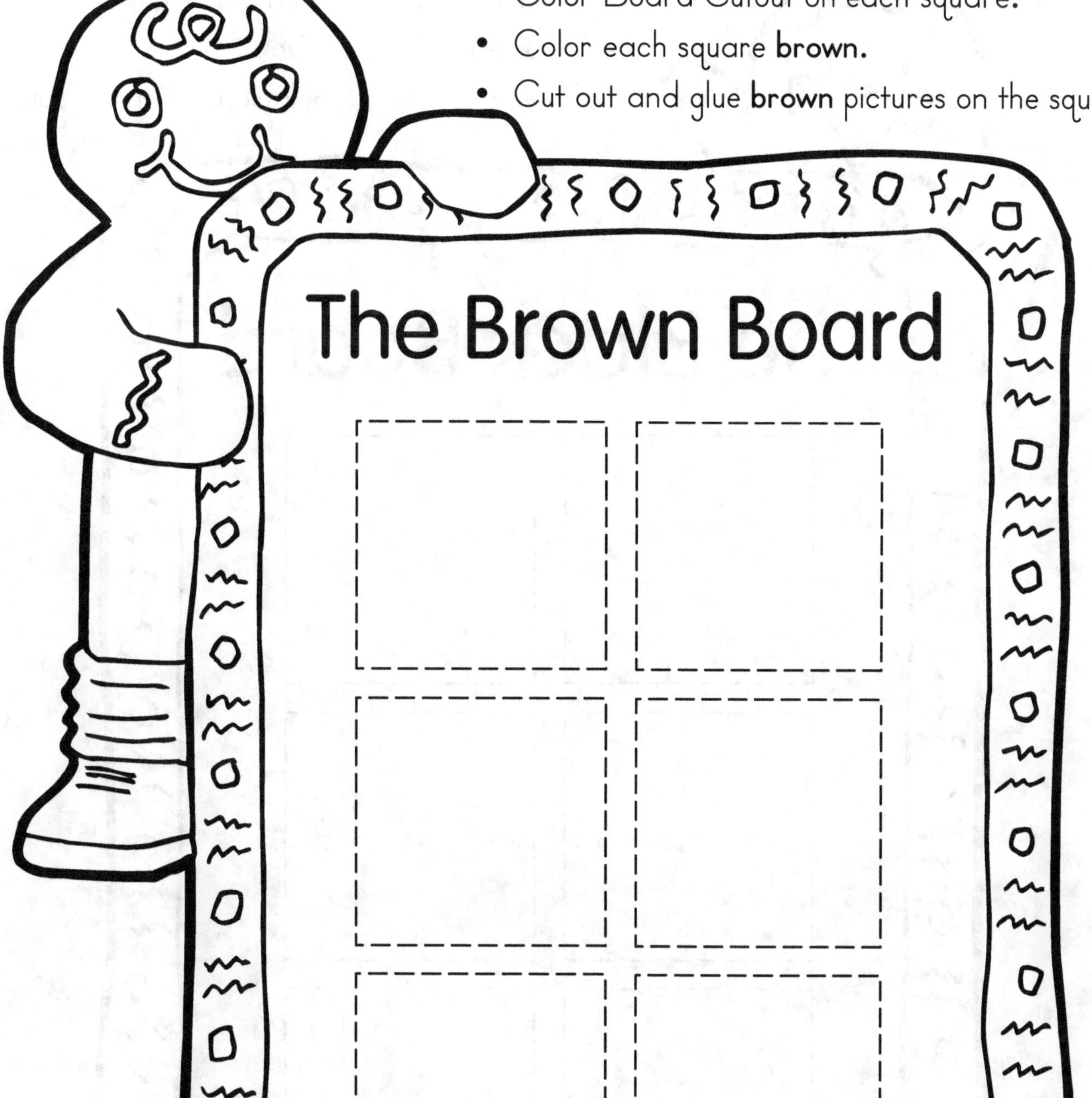

The Brown Board

© 2014 Little Acorn Books™

The Black Board

- Color, cut out and glue a **black** Color Board Cutout on each square.
- Color each square **black**.
- Cut out and glue **black** pictures on the squares.

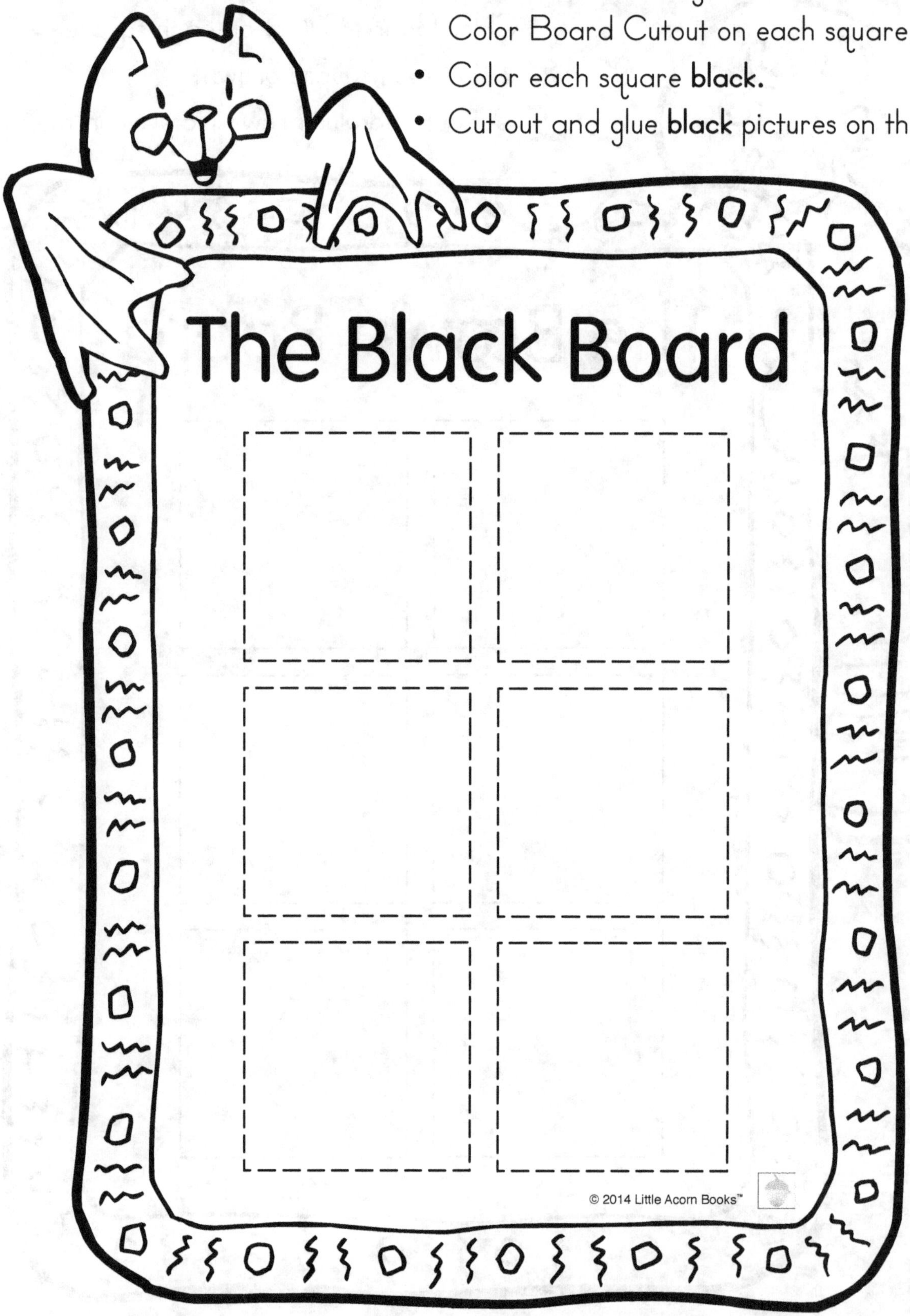

The Black Board

 LAB20147P • About Early Colors & Shapes • 978-1-937257-54-5 • © 2014 Little Acorn Books™

Color Board Cutouts

Reproduce colored construction paper color board cutouts. Reproduce enough cutouts of each color to fill each child's board. Children can work individually or in pairs to place matching color shapes on each color board (pages 40-46). Store the color boards and shapes in a decorated gift box.

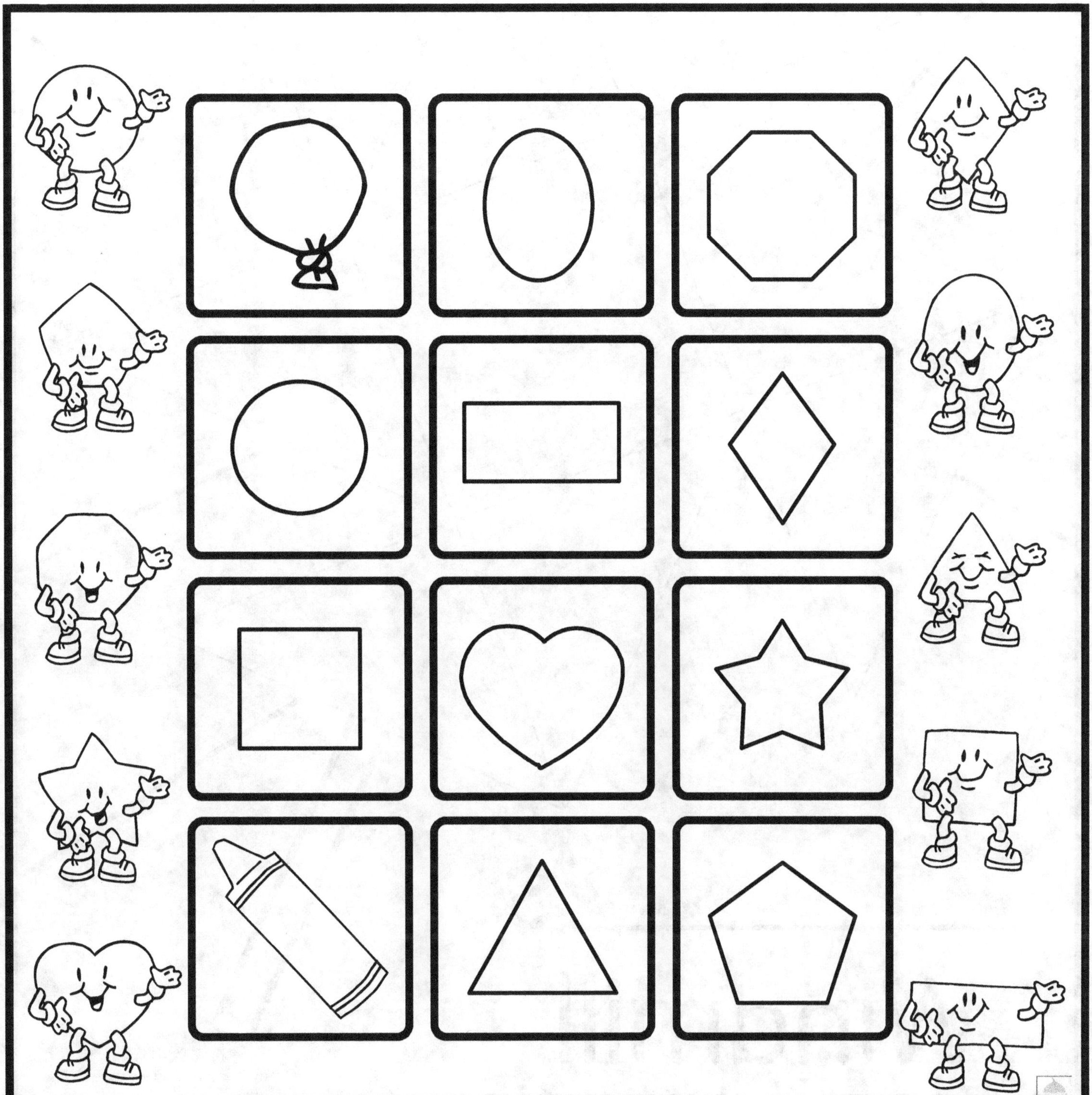

_____'s

Windmill

   LAB20147P • About Early Colors & Shapes • 978-1-937257-54-5 • © 2014 Little Acorn Books™

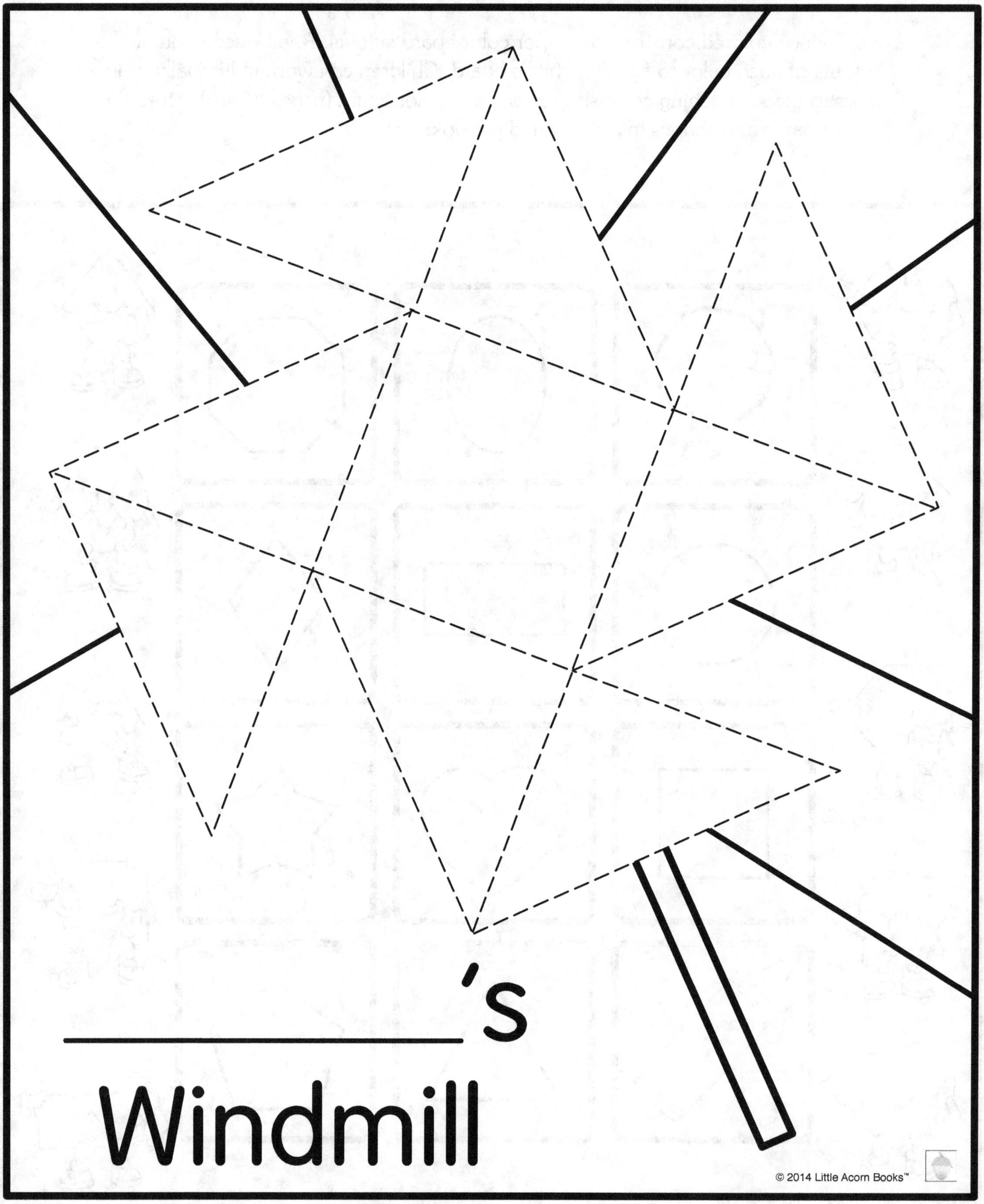

Windmill Tangram Puzzle Pieces

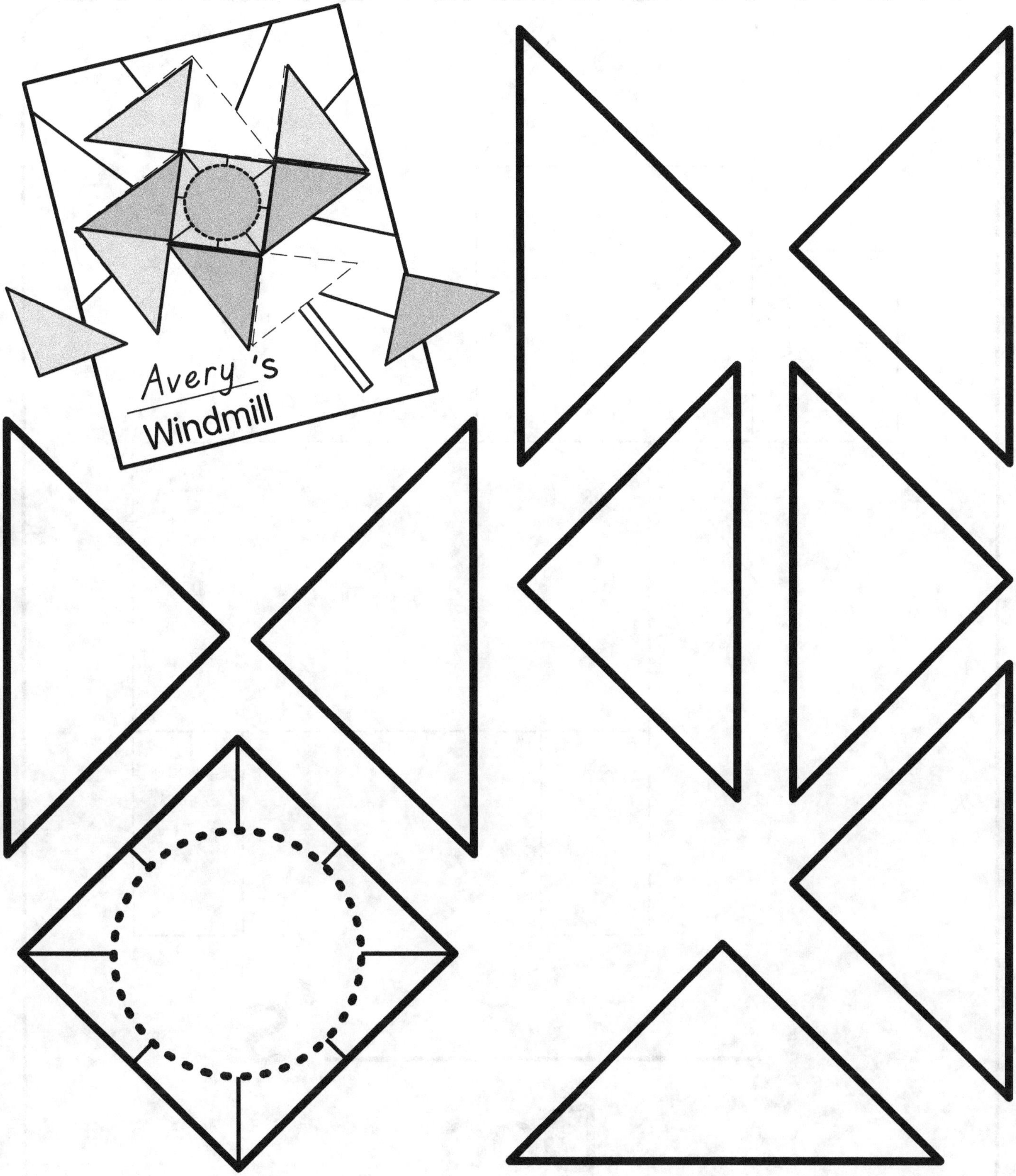

Avery's
Windmill

Dog Tangram Puzzle

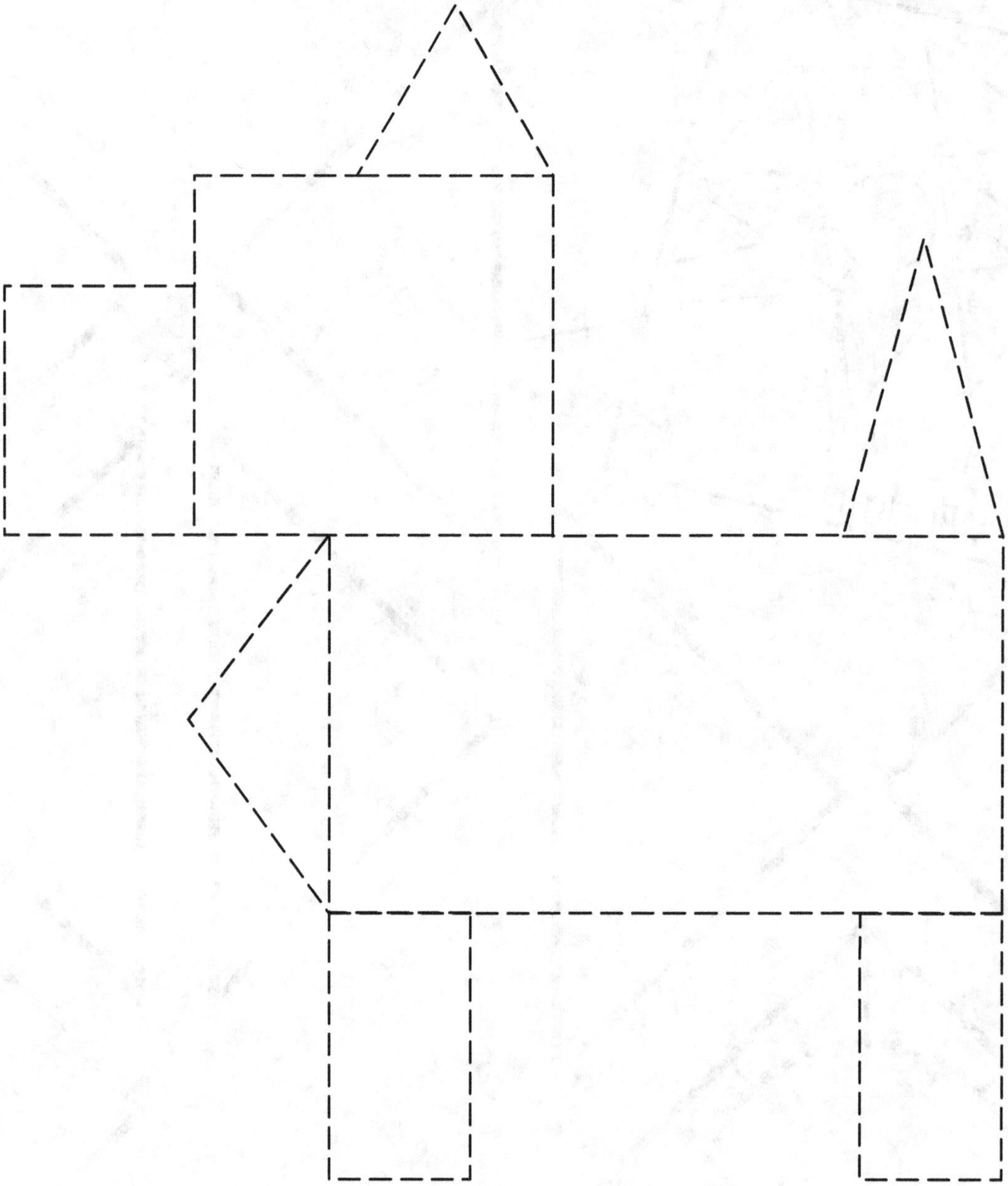

_____'s

Dog

LAB20147P • About Early Colors & Shapes • 978-1-937257-54-5 • © 2014 Little Acorn Books™

Dog Tangram Puzzle Pieces

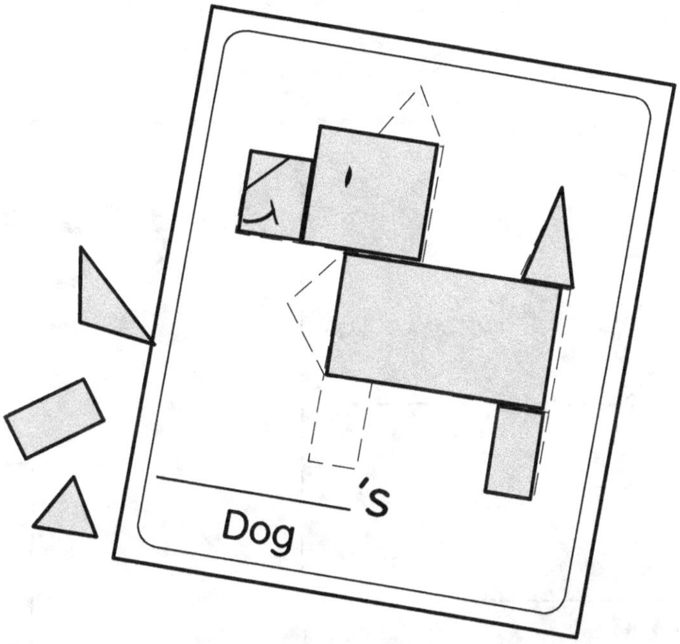

's

Dog

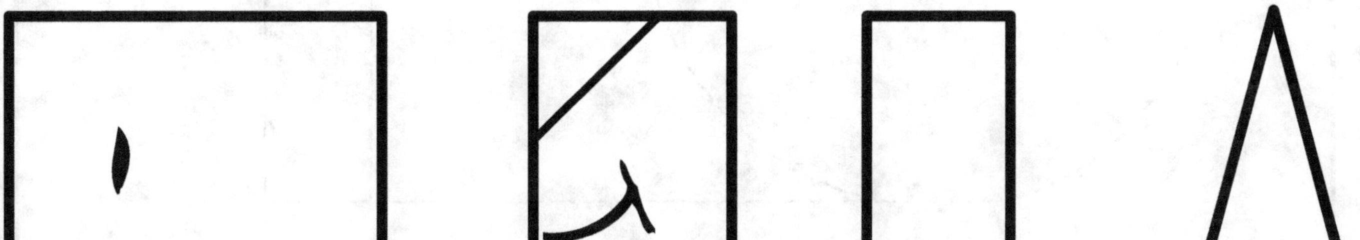

_____'s

Cat

 LAB20147P • About Early Colors & Shapes • 978-1-937257-54-5 • © 2014 Little Acorn Books™

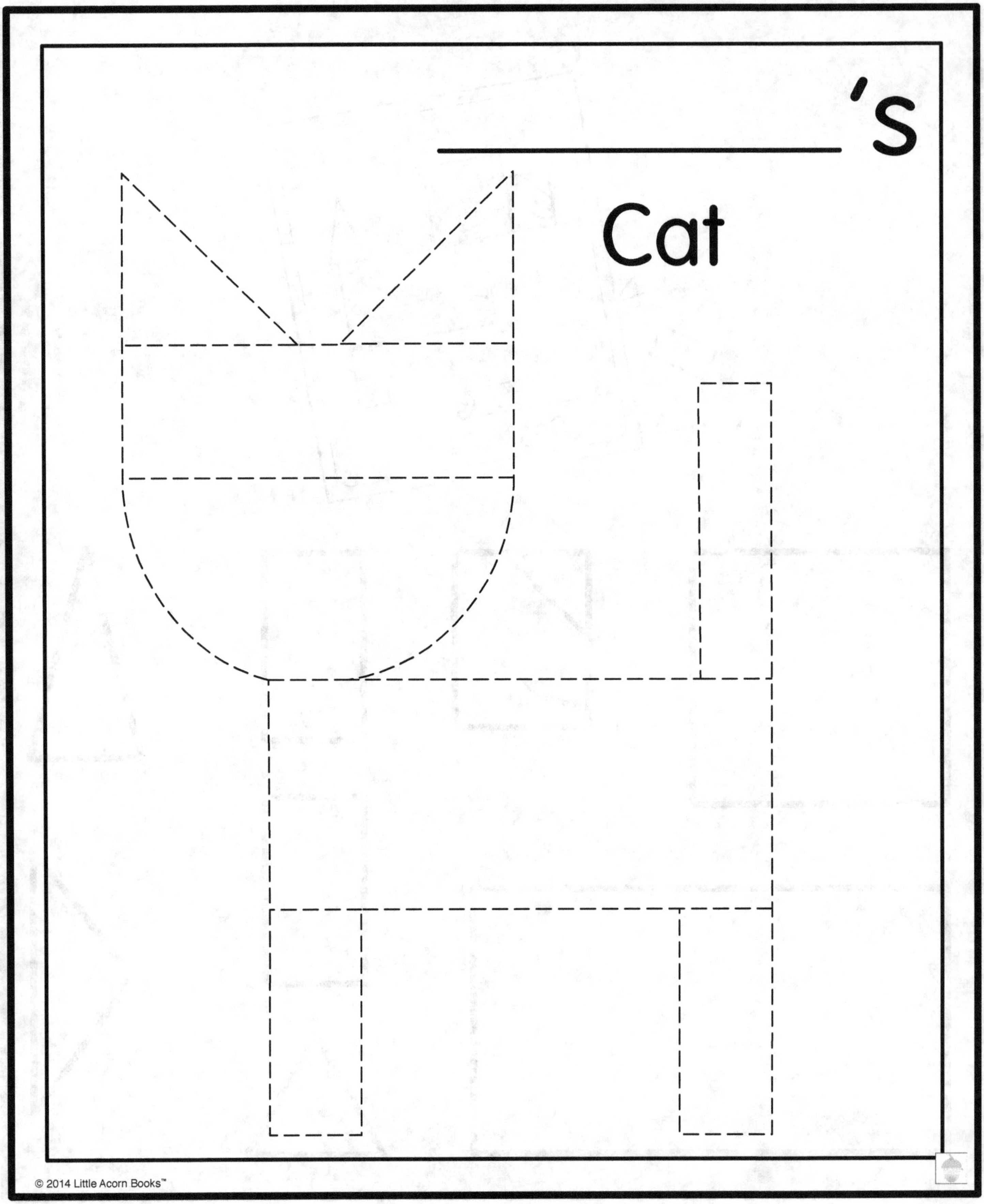

Cat Tangram Puzzle Pieces

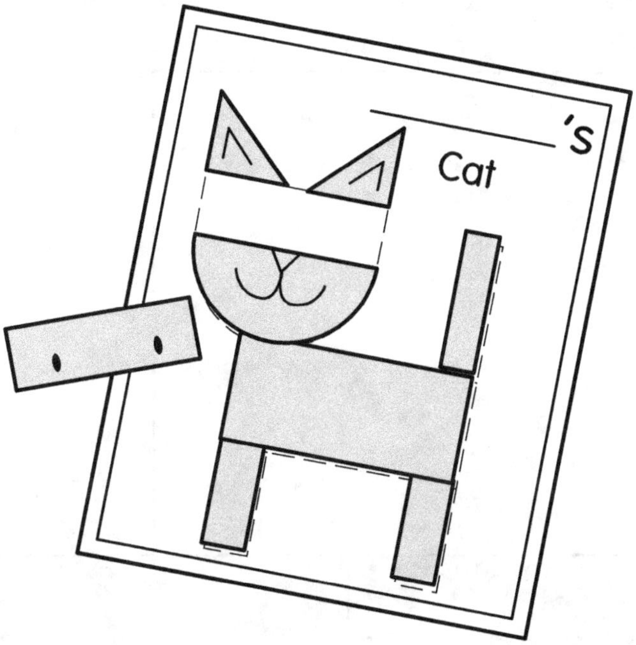

'S

Cat

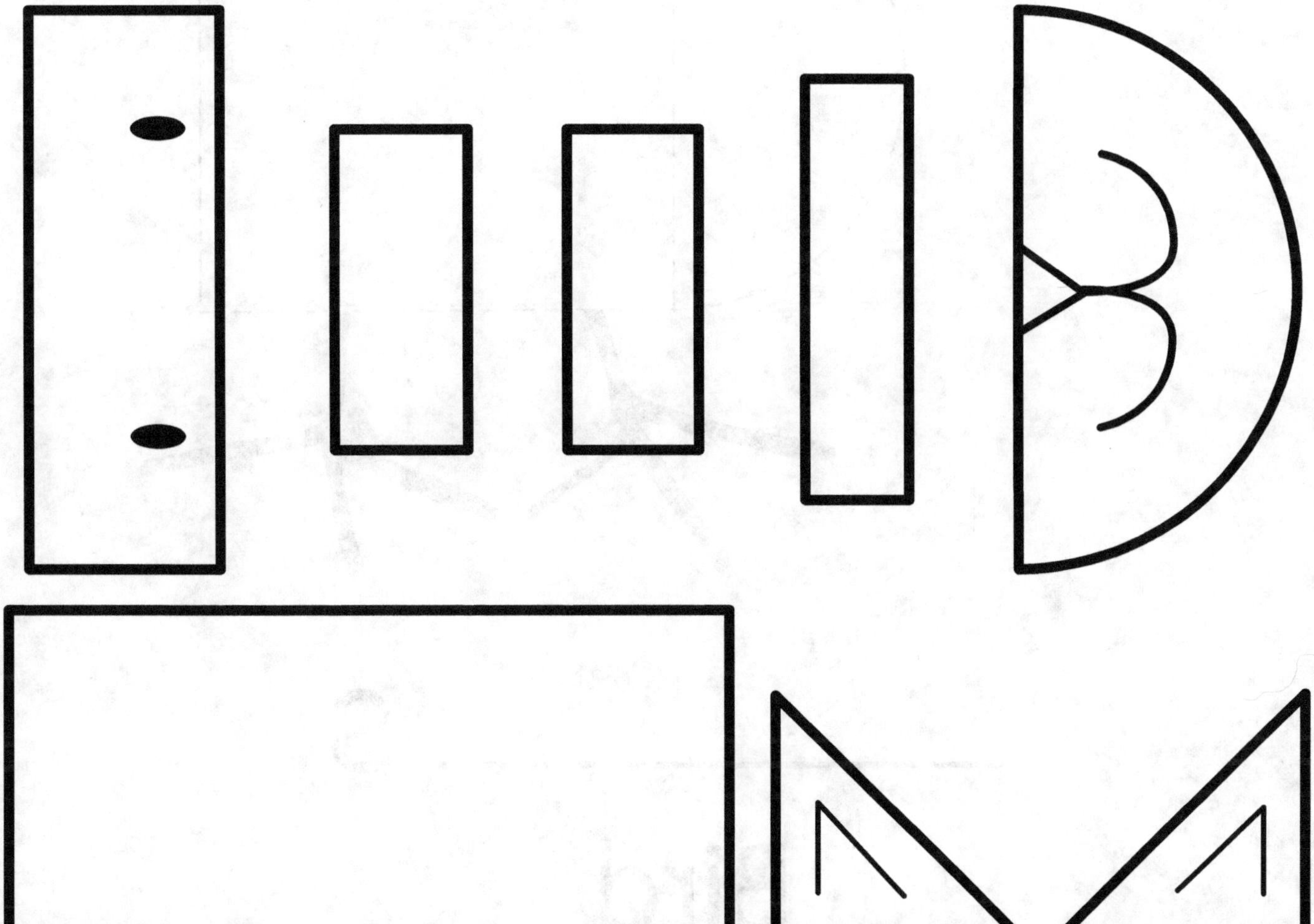

Bird Tangram Puzzle

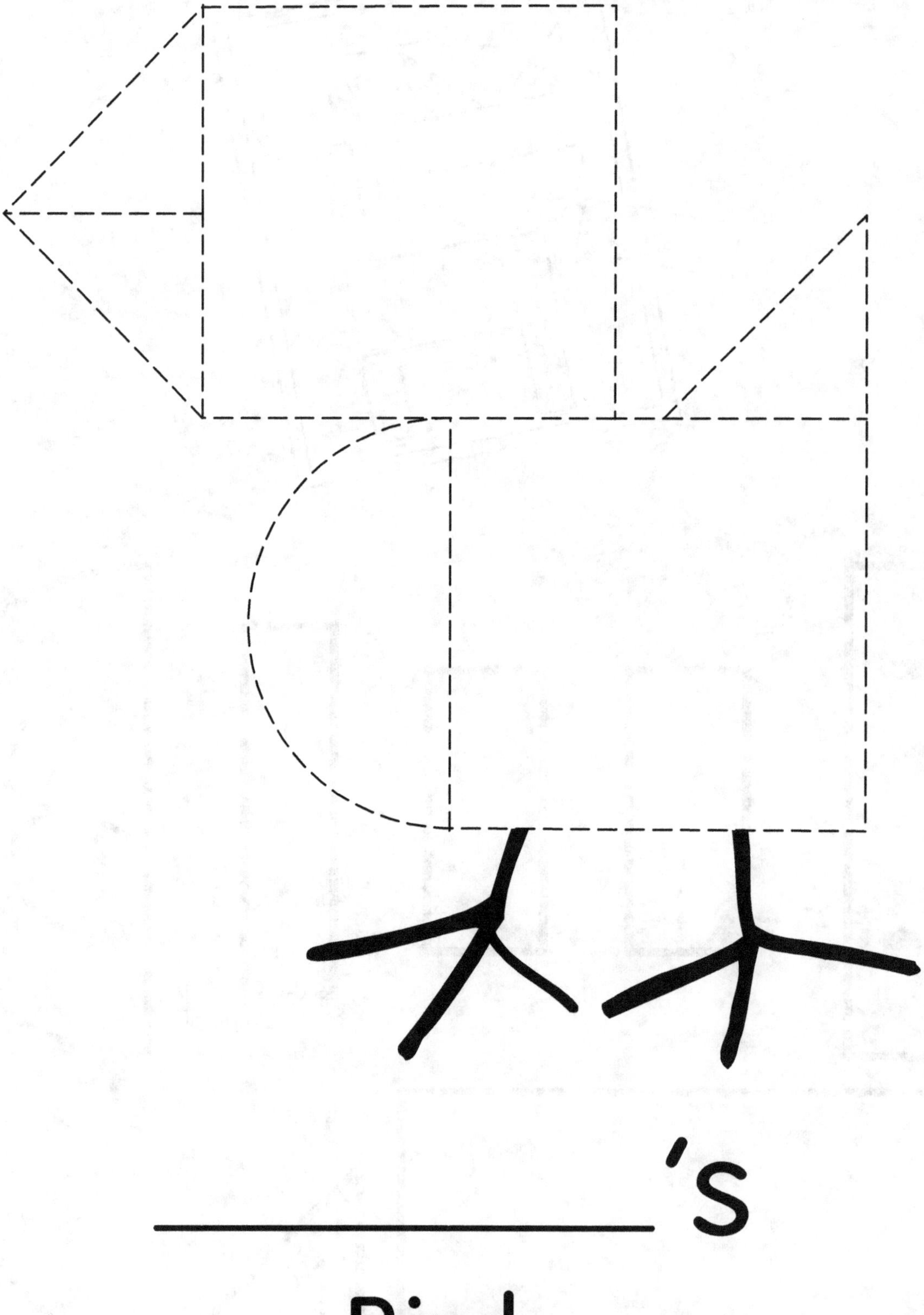

_____'s

Bird

 LAB20147P • *About Early Colors & Shapes* • 978-1-937257-54-5 • © 2014 Little Acorn Books™

Bird Tangram Puzzle Pieces

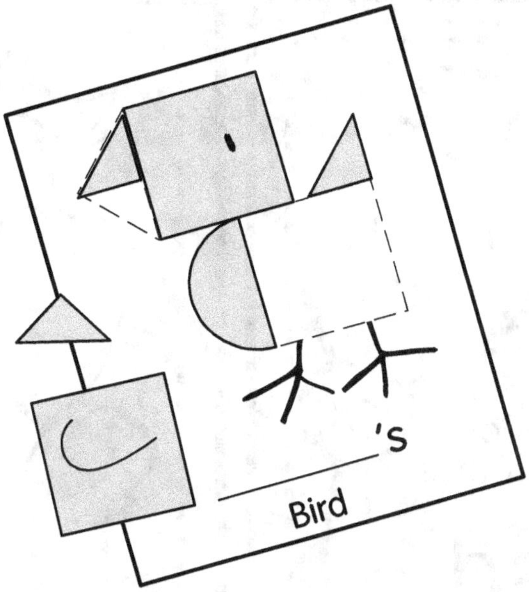

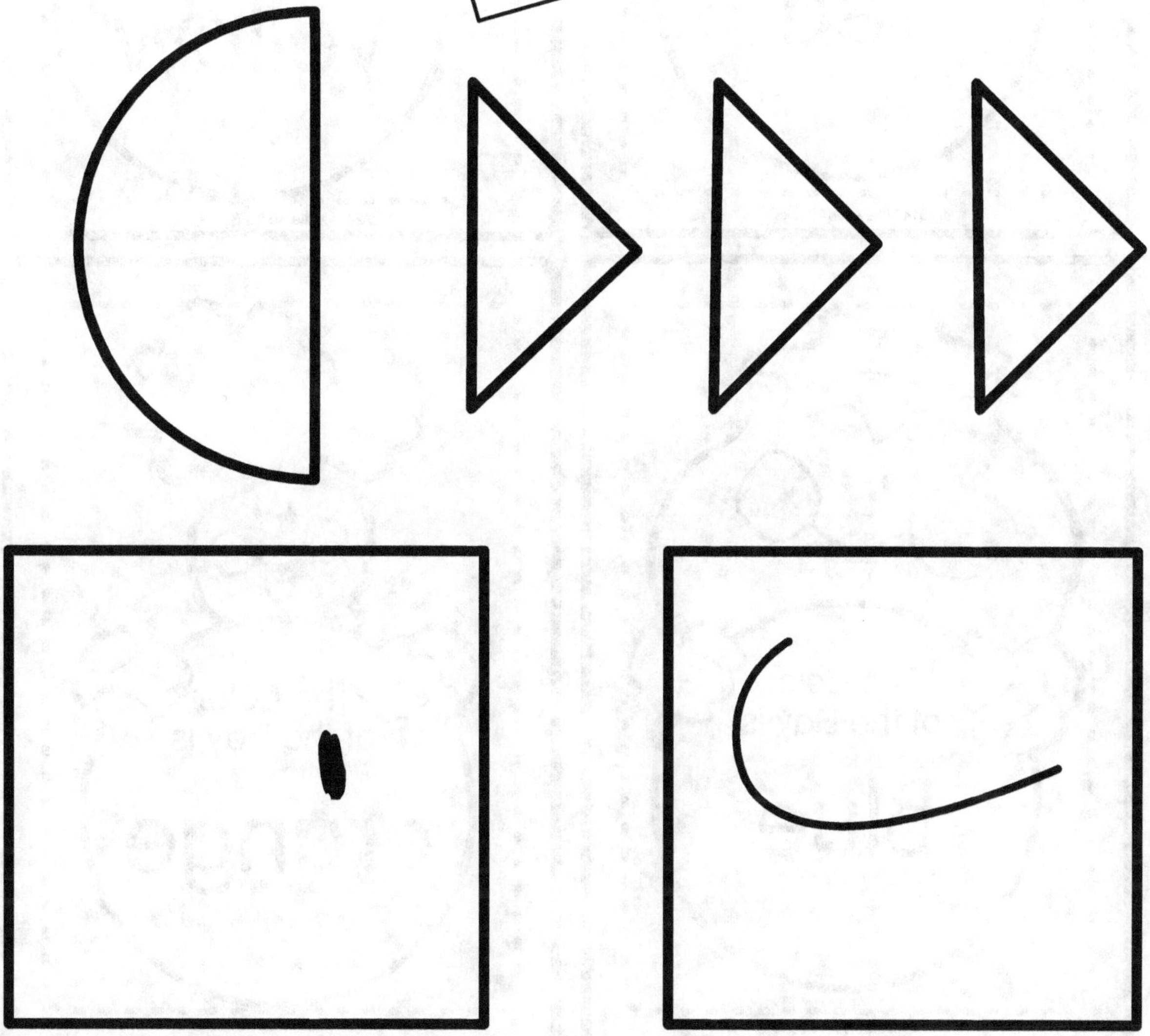

Bird's

Bird

Color of the Day Badges

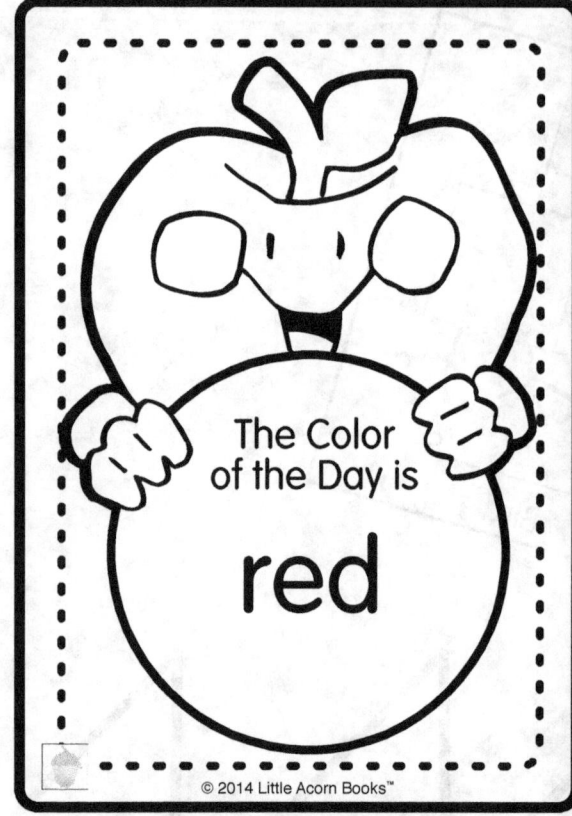

The Color of the Day is

red

© 2014 Little Acorn Books™

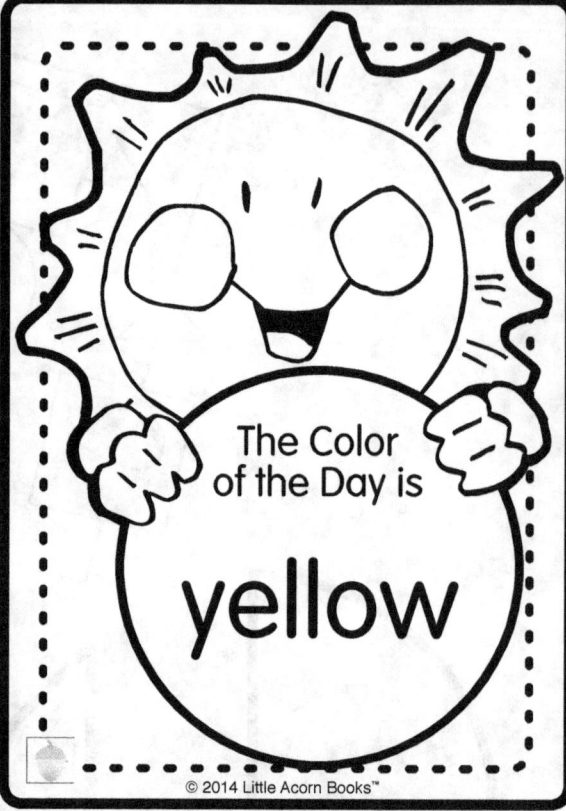

The Color of the Day is

yellow

© 2014 Little Acorn Books™

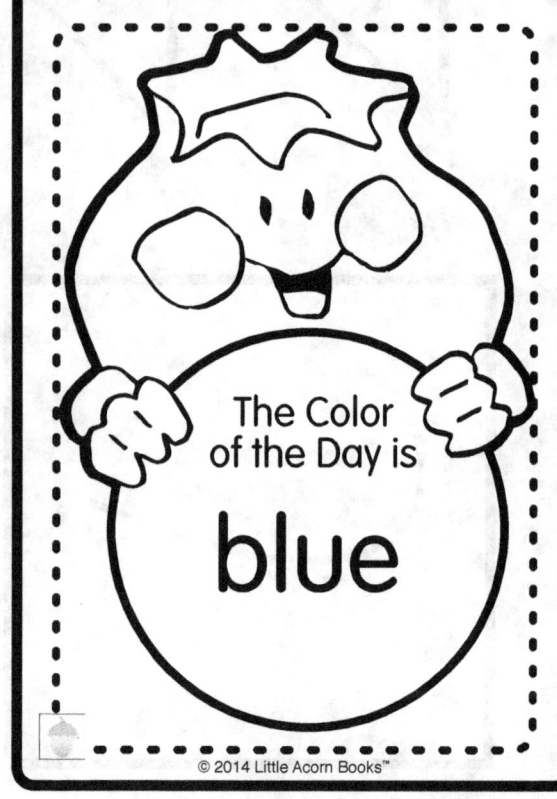

The Color of the Day is

blue

© 2014 Little Acorn Books™

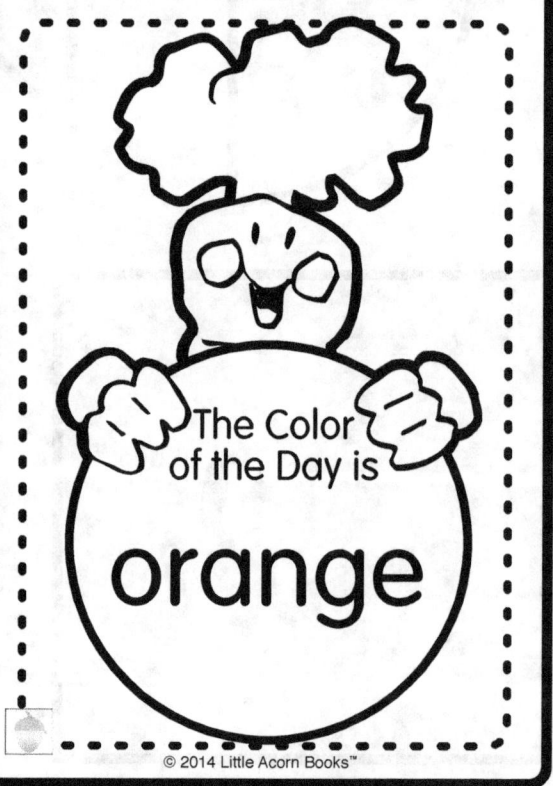

The Color of the Day is

orange

© 2014 Little Acorn Books™

LAB20147P • About Early Colors & Shapes • 978-1-937257-54-5 • © 2014 Little Acorn Books™

Color of the Day Badges

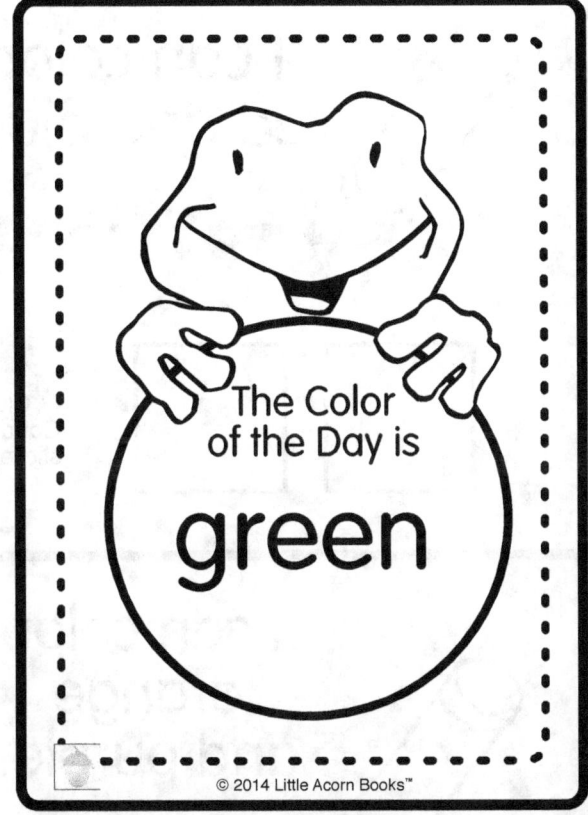

The Color of the Day is

green

© 2014 Little Acorn Books™

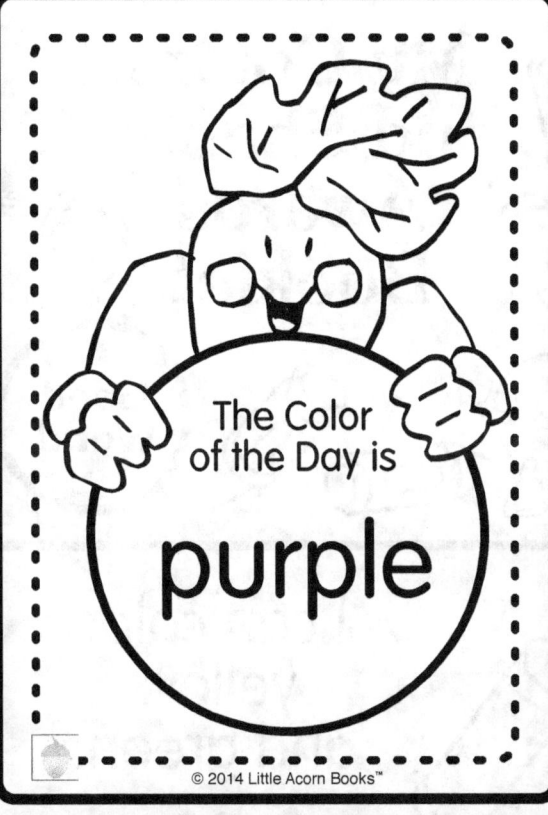

The Color of the Day is

purple

© 2014 Little Acorn Books™

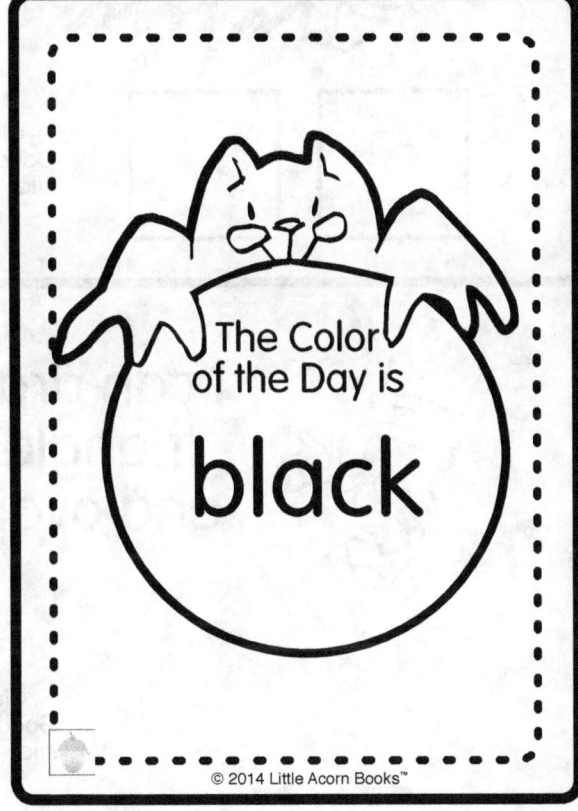

The Color of the Day is

black

© 2014 Little Acorn Books™

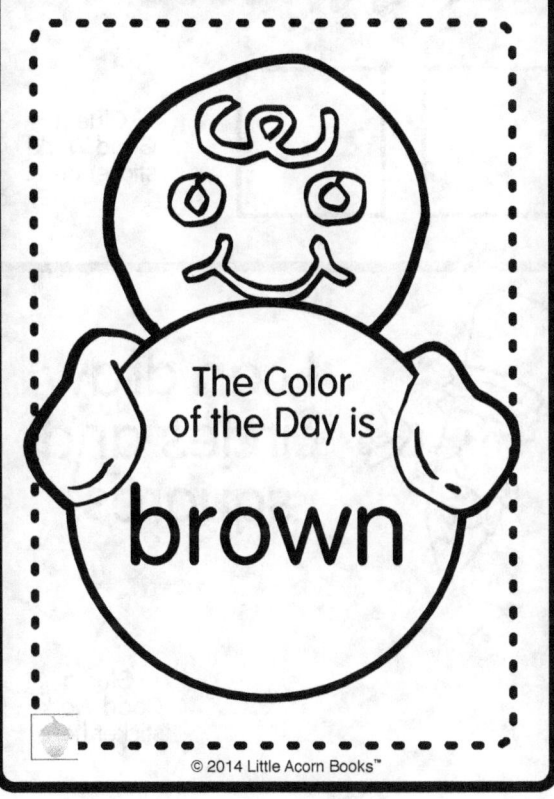

The Color of the Day is

brown

© 2014 Little Acorn Books™

Awards Booklet

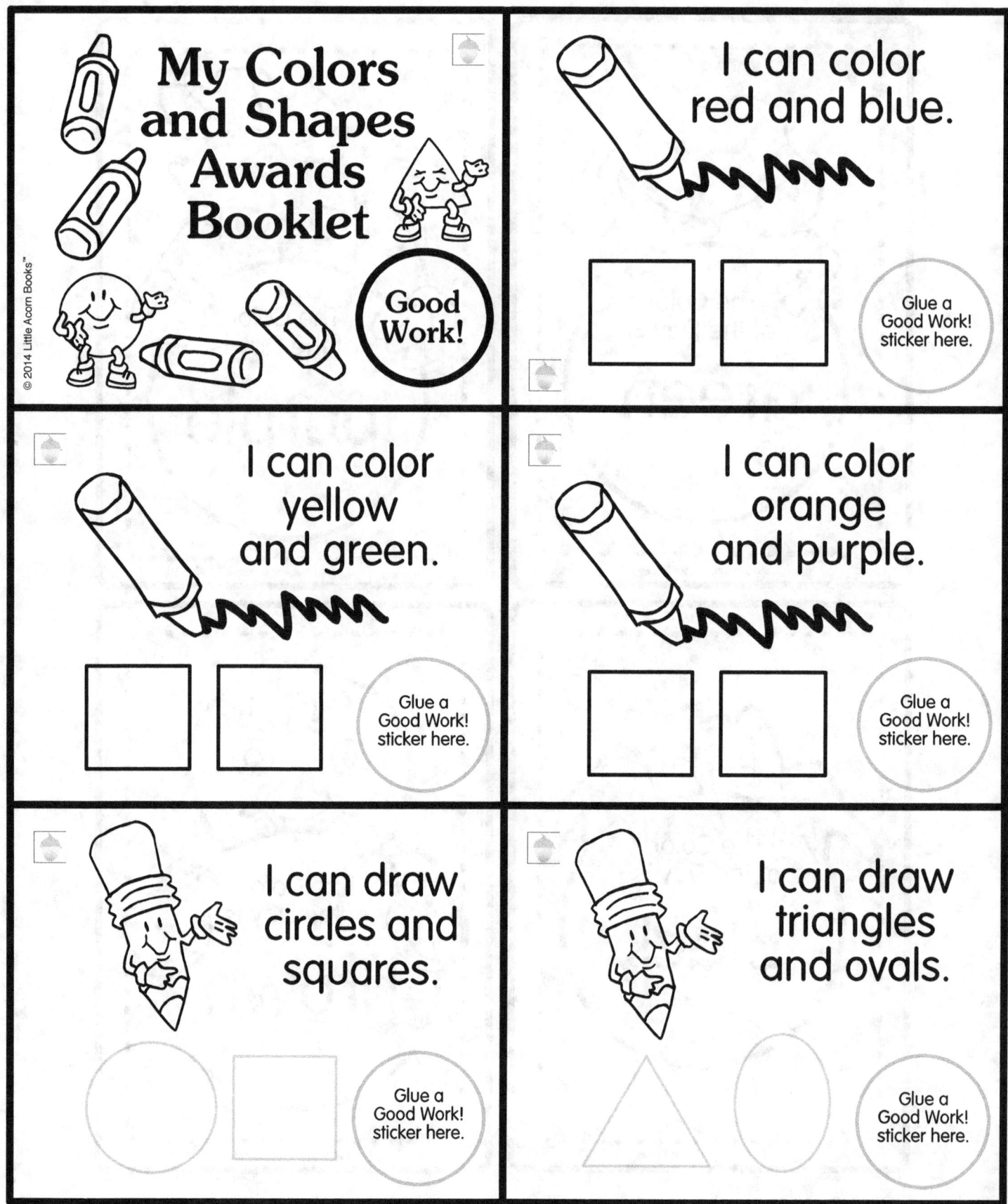

My Colors and Shapes Awards Booklet

Good Work!

© 2014 Little Acorn Books™

I can color red and blue.

Glue a Good Work! sticker here.

I can color yellow and green.

Glue a Good Work! sticker here.

I can color orange and purple.

Glue a Good Work! sticker here.

I can draw circles and squares.

Glue a Good Work! sticker here.

I can draw triangles and ovals.

Glue a Good Work! sticker here.

LAB20147P • About Early Colors & Shapes • 978-1-937257-54-5 • © 2014 Little Acorn Books™

Awards Booklet

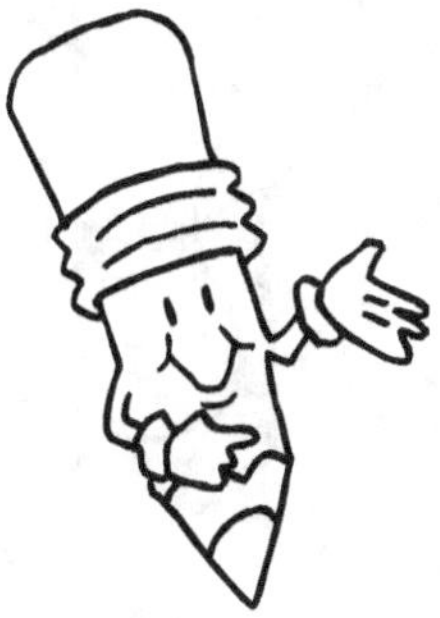

I can draw pentagons and octagons.

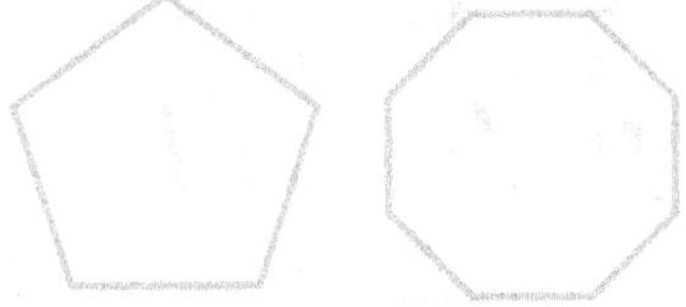

Glue a Good Work! sticker here.

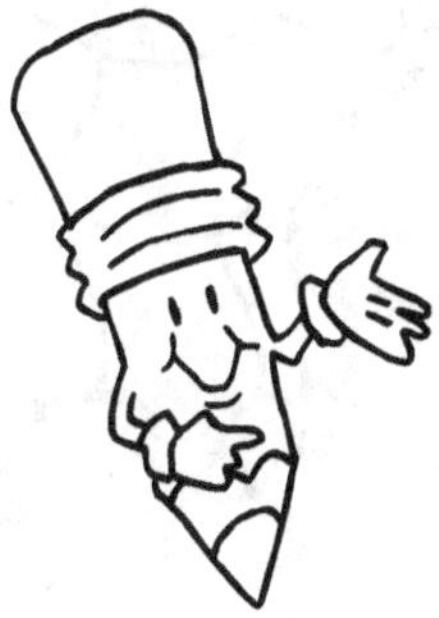

I can draw rectangles and diamonds.

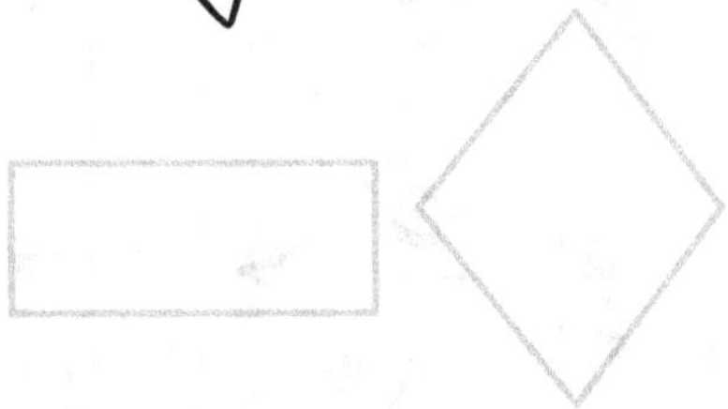

Glue a Good Work! sticker here.

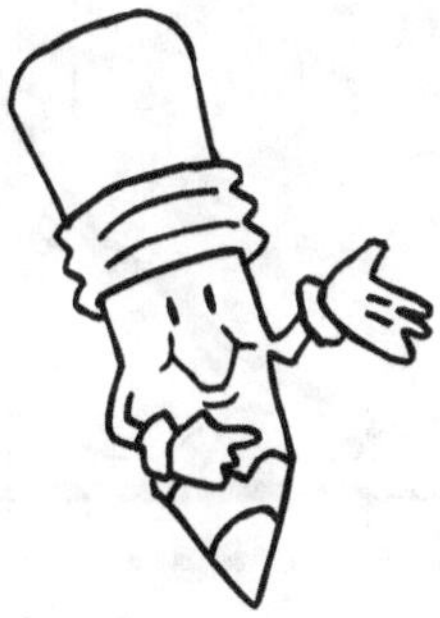

I can draw stars and hearts.

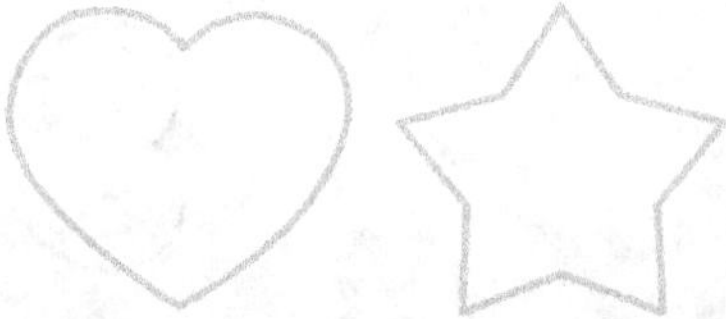

Glue a Good Work! sticker here.

I can cut out shapes.

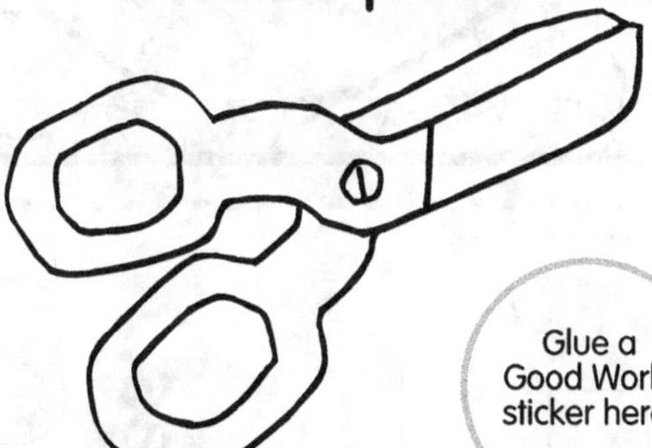

Glue a Good Work! sticker here.

Good Work! Good Work! Good Work! Good Work! Good Work!

Good Work! Good Work! Good Work! Good Work! Good Work!

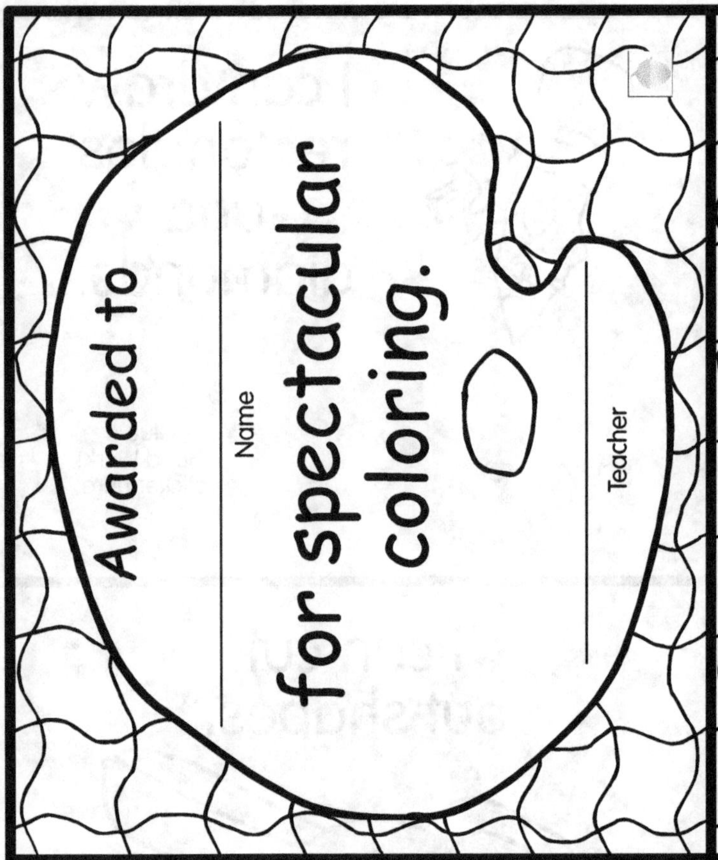

Awarded to

_____
Name

for spectacular coloring.

_____
Teacher

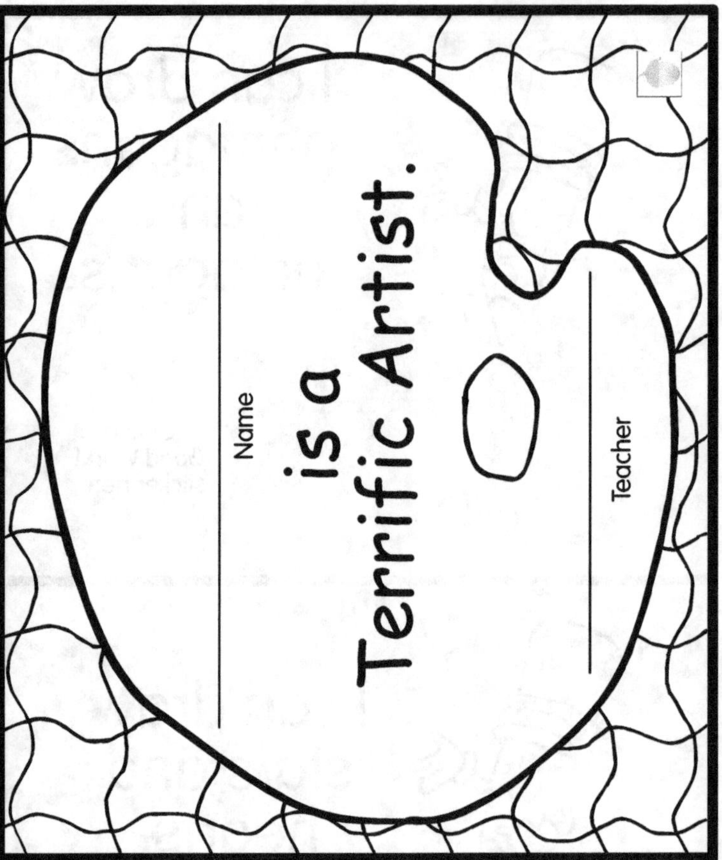

_____
Name

is a Terrific Artist.

_____
Teacher

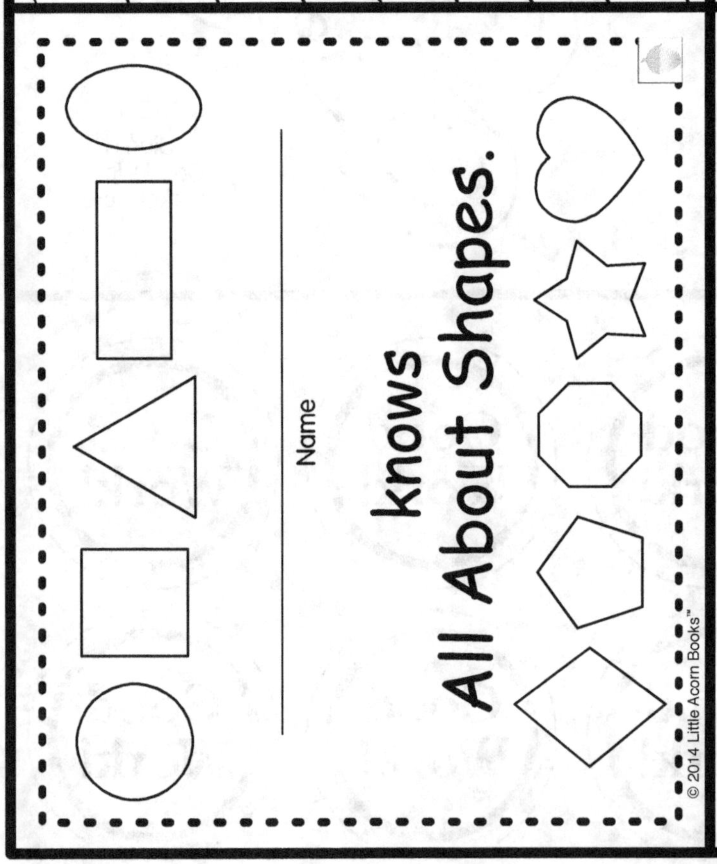

_____
Name

knows All About Shapes.

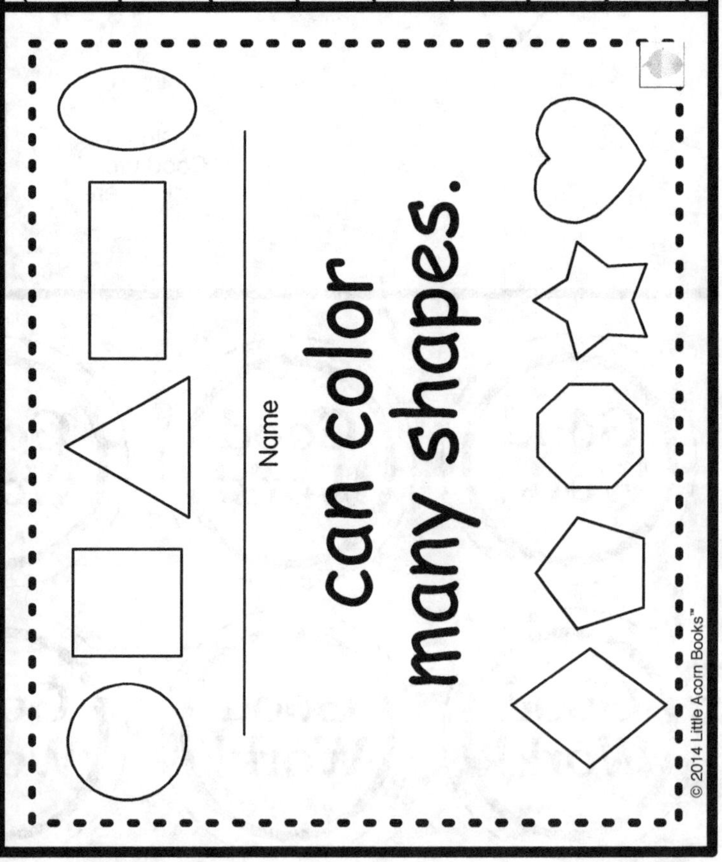

_____
Name

can color many shapes.

Take-home Notes

Dear Parent,
We are learning about the shapes listed below.

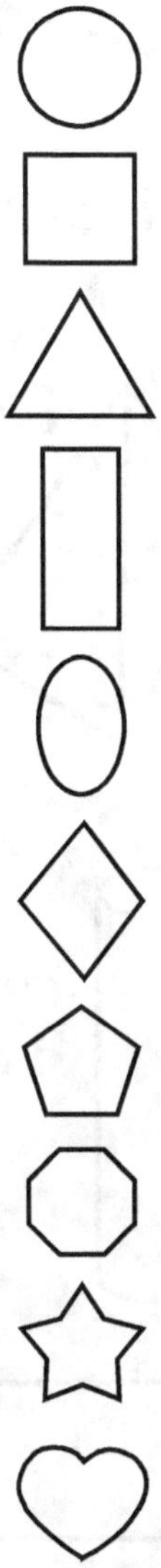

○ circles

□ squares

△ triangles

▭ rectangles

⬭ ovals

◇ diamonds

⬠ pentagons

⯃ octagons

☆ stars

♡ hearts

Please help your child identify matching shapes around the house.

_____
Teacher

Dear Parent,
We are learning about the colors listed below.

red

yellow

blue

green

orange

purple

brown

black

Please help your child choose a matching color object to bring for show and tell.

_____
Teacher

More Colors and Shapes

Color each paintbrush, then write the matching color word on the handle.

More Colors

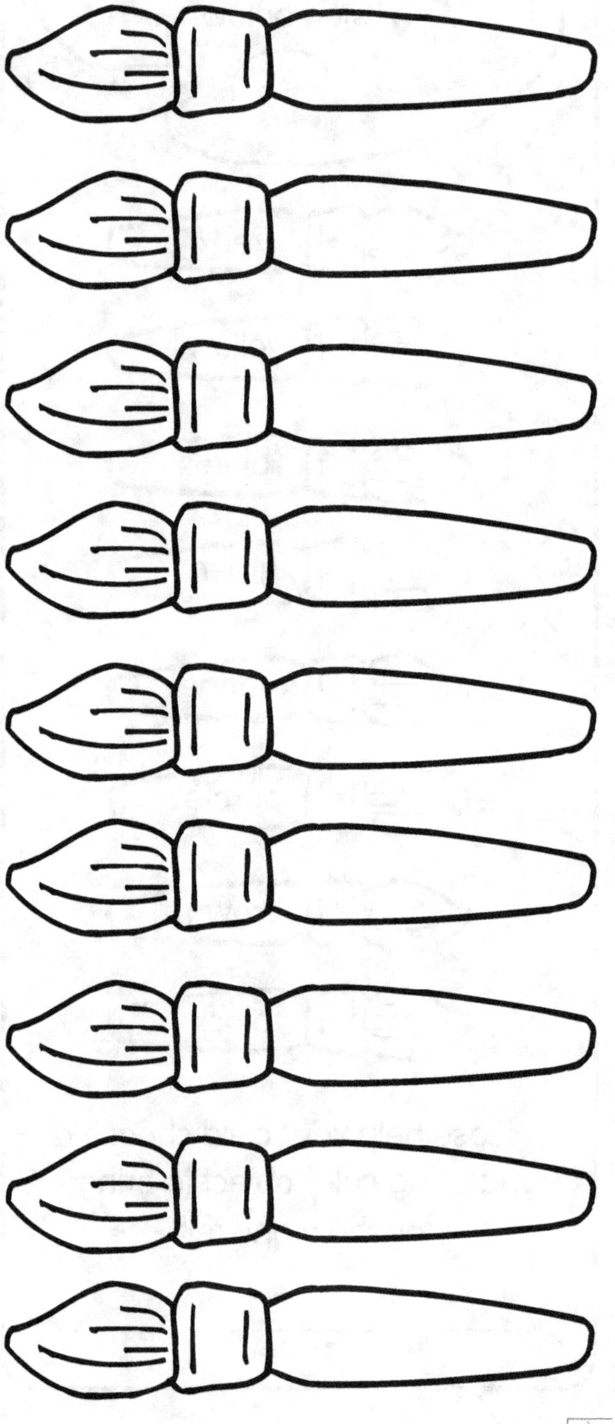

More Shapes

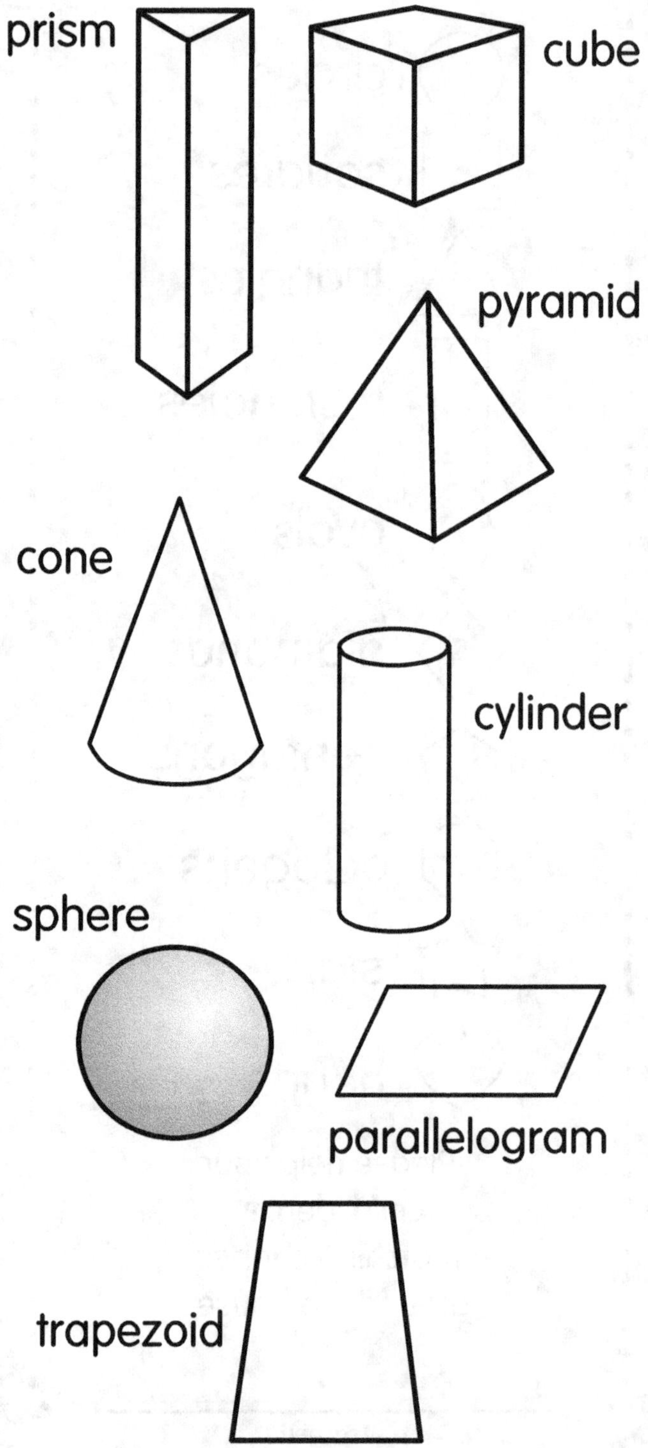

prism

cube

pyramid

cone

cylinder

sphere

parallelogram

trapezoid

 LAB20147P • About Early Colors & Shapes • 978-1-937257-54-5 • © 2014 Little Acorn Books™

Piglet Paint Jars

Reproduce two sets and color each piglet paint jar a different color
(red, yellow, blue, green, orange, purple, black, and brown).

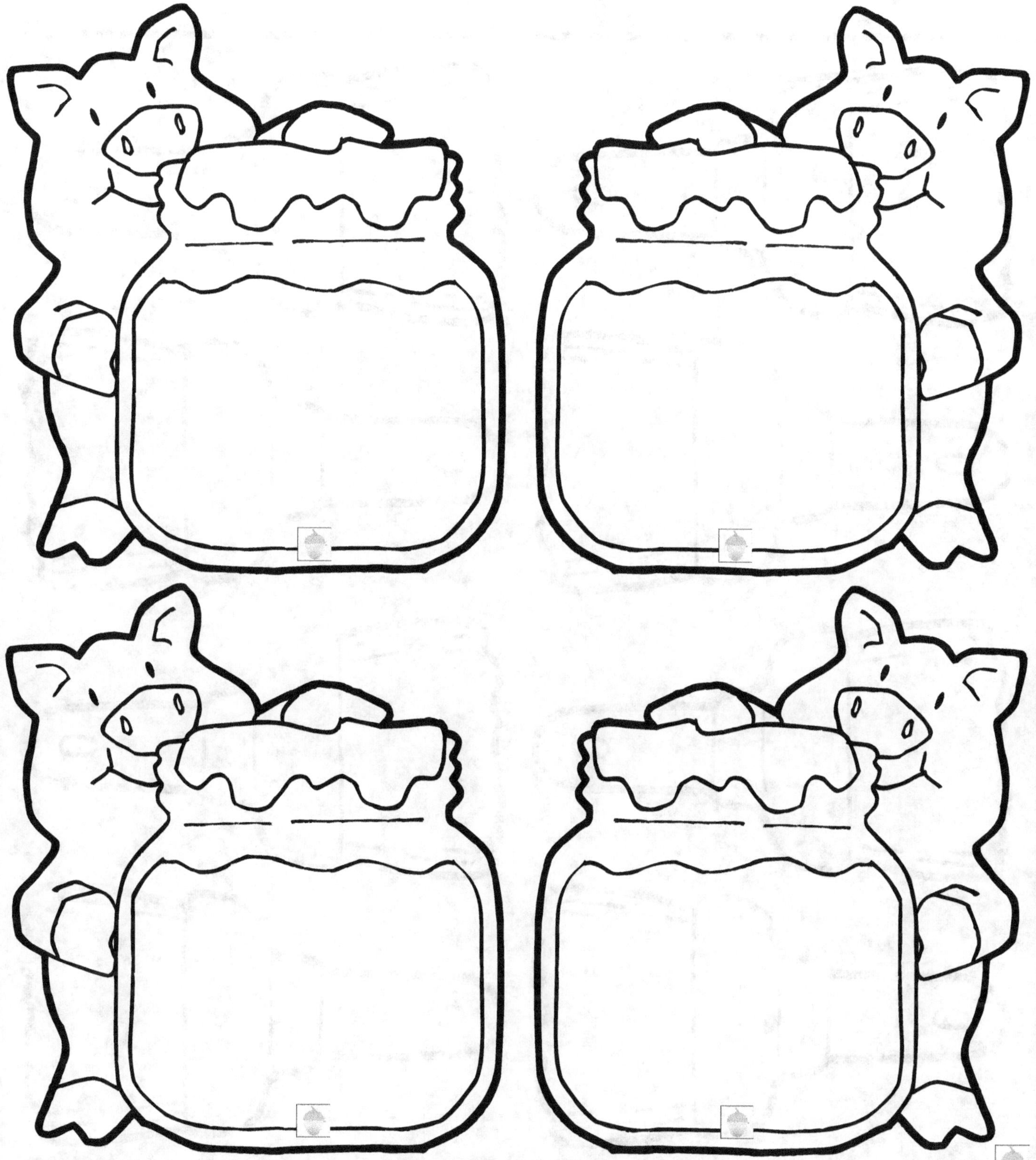

Piglet Paintbrushes

Reproduce and color each paintbrush pattern a different color (red, yellow, blue, green, orange, purple, black, and brown). Write the matching color word on the back of each paintbrush. Then laminate and cut out the paintbrushes. Store the paintbrushes in a resealable plastic bag.

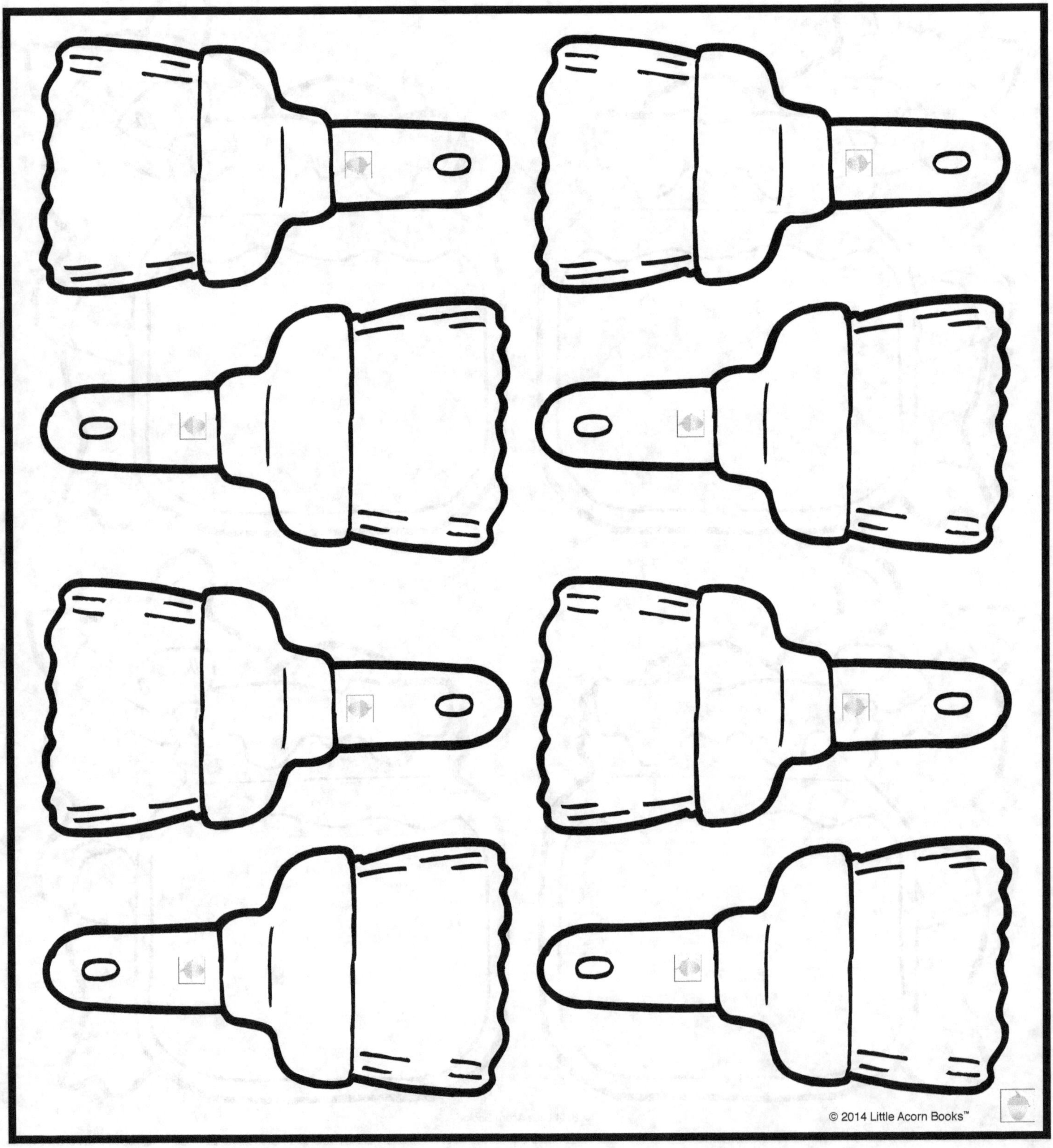

LAB20147P • About Early Colors & Shapes • 978-1-937257-54-5 • © 2014 Little Acorn Books™

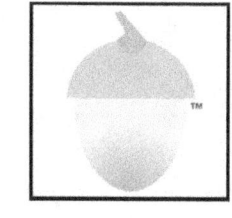

Little Acorn Books™

Promoting Early Skills for a Lifetime™

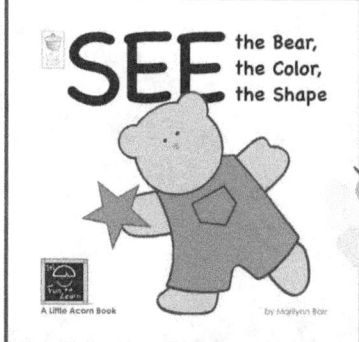 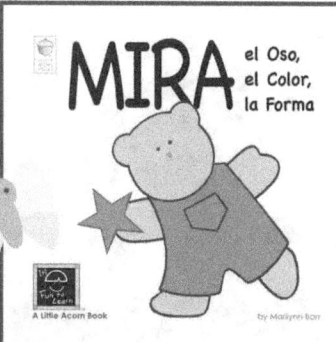 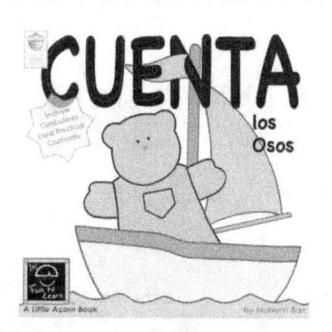 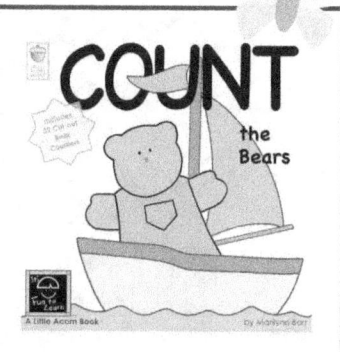

A Hands-on Picture Book Series • Infancy–Age 4

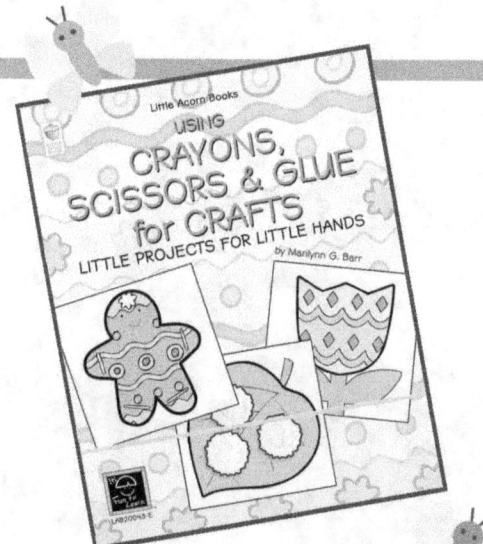

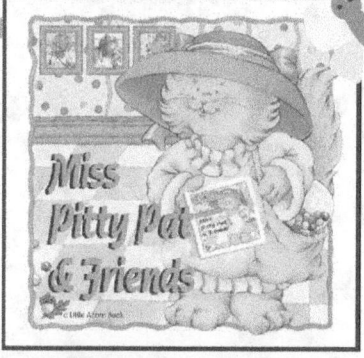

Miss Pitty Pat & Friends
Preschool–Grade 1

Using Crayons, Scissors, & Glue for Crafts
Preschool–Grade 1

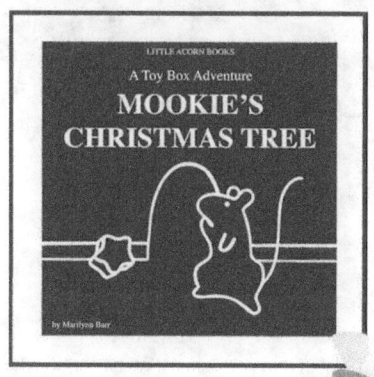

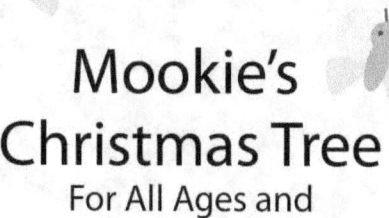

Mookie's Christmas Tree
For All Ages and
Not Just for Christmas

Little Acorn Books™
Visit our web site:
www.littleacornbooks.com